MANAGING ACROSS SECTORS:

Similarities And Differences Between For-Profit and Voluntary Non-Profit Organisations

DR DIANA LEAT
Visiting Senior Research Fellow
VOLPROF

City University Business School

March 1993

Contents

Summary of Supposed Differences Between Non-profit and For-profit Organisations

NON-PROFIT ORGANISATIONS	FOR-PROFIT ORGANISATIONS
1. Not concerned with profit	**Driven by profit maximisation**

Reality

a. In both sectors 'profit' is an unclear concept. Its meaning and measurement vary.

b. Some non-profits and parts of others generate profit/surplus - even if they cannot distribute that profit.

c. The timescale over which for-profit organisations attempt to maximise profit varies.

d. It is debatable whether profit maximisation is the primary goal for all types of for-profit organisation in all types of market. Maximising sales and/or growth may be equally, if not more, important.

2. Difficulties in raising capital because of lack of profit distribution	**Able to raise capital on the basis of assets and prospects**

Reality

a. Some non-profits are able to raise capital in grants rather than loans. Reputation and current budget are likely to be more important in securing a grant; assets may be a disadvantage.

b. Small for-profit organisations, in particular, may have difficulty in raising capital.

c. One of the greatest difficulties for both non-profit and for-profit organisations in their early years is ensuring sufficient capitalisation.

3. No risk	**Always entail financial risk**

Reality

a. Risk, financial and other, may be experienced by both for-profit and non-profit organisations.

b. The financial liability of for-profit entrepreneurs is likely to be hedged by financial institutions, whereas in non-profits risk may be less well insured.

4. Lack of profit as a bottom line deprives the organisation of any basis for performance indicators	**Profit provides the basis for clear performance indicators**

Reality

a. Profit is problematic as a concept and as a basis for measurement of performance in for-profit organisations (see above point 1.).

b. Profit may be an inadequate/inappropriate basis for measuring performance in parts of for-profit organisations, e.g. service departments. Intangible or indirect contributions to the achievement of goals are what is difficult to measure in both sectors.

c. But inability to distribute profit may indeed create difficulties for non-profits in introducing performance related pay by means of, for example, stock options and profit-sharing plans.

5.	**Non-competitive**	**Inherently competitive**

Reality

a. Perfect competition among for-profit organisations rarely exists outside economics textbooks. In the for-profit sector there are monopolies, oligopolies and co-operation between organisations to protect or further common interests.

b. Non-profit organisations compete with each other for donors, contracts and dominance in market niches.

c. But competition among non-profit organisations must take into account:
   (i) the public perception of charities as dedicated to the pursuit of public benefit rather than establishing organisational dominance;
   (ii) the impossibility of hostile take-overs and the difficulties in friendly mergers;
   (iii) what is regarded in the for-profit sector as healthy competition promoting choice for consumers may be viewed as wasteful duplication in the non-profit sector. For this reason, establishing a distinctive market niche may be equally important to both types of organisation.

6.	**No direct link between funder and customer/consumer.** **Paid for efforts**	**Direct link between funder and customer/consumer.** **Paid for results**

Reality

a. The notion of the 'customer' is fundamentally woolly, concealing important distinctions between types/levels of customers and end-users. In both sectors the definition and identification of customers are problematic.

b. In some non-profit organisations or in some activities/services the funder and customer/consumer *are* one and the same.

c. In both for-profit and non-profit organisations the funder customer and the end-user consumer may be different.

d. In both for-profit and non-profit organisations consumer demand may be an inadequate guide to measurement of quality performance because of the nature of the product or the structure of the market.

e. Both types of organisation may face theoretical and practical problems in 'staying close to the customer/end-user'.

7.	**Governed by a Board of unremunerated trustees representing diverse interests**	**Managers paid to manage. Board and managers share same goals**

Reality

a. Non-profit trustees may fulfil the same function as non-executive directors in for-profit organisations.

b. In larger for-profits, Boards are likely to represent diverse and dispersed minority and majority, individual and institutional shareholder interests.

c. In both types of organisation Board members may have neither the time nor the knowledge to challenge managers.

d. In both types of organisation research suggests that managers are able to structure the information received by the Board. Managers may 'lead' the Board rather than vice versa.

8. Charitable status requires substantive, usually intangible, mission. Organisation cannot change mission without serious damage to raison d'etre	One tangible objective: profit maximisation. Organisation may change goals and methods as long as it continues to deliver profits

Reality

a. For good legal reasons charitable missions tend to be broad enough to allow considerable flexibility in practice. Many charities have been adept at re-defining their missions to ensure survival.

b. Some for-profit organisations have similarly broad intangible objectives – such as quality for the customer – even if one measure of success is then sales and/or profit (see above for further comments on profit as a central goal).

9. Management problems due to preponderance of professionals/ knowledge workers and volunteers	Clear structures of authority and control using payment as reward and sanction

Reality

a. Many for-profit organisations are increasingly dominated by professionals and knowledge workers who demand a high degree of autonomy in their work. Managing professionals and knowledge workers constitutes a challenge for both non-profit and for-profit organisations.

b. In order to recruit and retain staff in future both types of organisation may have to rely less on pay and more on total packages of wider benefits and satisfactions.

c. Non-profit organisations may face particular difficulties in offering attractive employment packages because:

    (i) many non-profits are not free to determine their own pay levels or even to follow the market. Charities may be further constrained by public expectations of 'appropriate' pay and benefit levels.

    (ii) non-profit organisations may have difficulty in offering other benefits because of their cost, what the funder will accept and chronic insecurity of funding. Job security may present particular problems.

    (iii) many non-profits may be constrained by organisational values which stress equality rather than differentials.

4. Non-profits involving volunteers may have much to teach for-profits in providing satisfactions and rewards other than pay. But a commitment to volunteer involvement may create particular management difficulties in:

    (i) relating performance to rewards for both paid and unpaid staff;

    (ii) applying performance evaluation and standards;

    (iii) encouraging provision of jobs for people rather than people for jobs.

10. Ethos of participation and equality	Hierarchical, non-democratic, managed organisations

Reality

a. Both for-profit and non-profit organisations are required to implement basic equal opportunities legislation. But non-profit organisations may experience particular pressures because:

    (i) they may be expected to be more equal than others;

    (ii) in non-profit organisations equal opportunities may be as much a matter of process as of results;

    (iii) non-profit organisations may have particular difficulties in meeting the costs of implementing equal opportunities policy.

b. A wider commitment to equality and participation, beyond equal opportunities, is not characteristic of all non-profit organisations.

c. Some for-profit organisations may also display egalitarian and participative characteristics. New technologies may require greater worker autonomy and participation. In addition, many of the new management texts argue that equality and participation are essential paths to quality, innovation and success.

11. Accountable to a wide variety of constituencies | Only one constituency matters – the customer

Reality

a. Depending on the type of organisation, its market and social and political environment, for-profits' constituencies may be many and varied.

b. The number and diversity of constituencies to which a non-profit organisation is accountable will vary depending in part on the degree of organisational slack, the organisation's need for, and possible sources of, legitimacy and the power, visibility and vocality of constituents themselves.

c. In both types of organisation accountability may be confused by lack of clarity over whose interests the organisation/Board exists to serve (e.g. employees, funders, members, customers, potential customers) and over what timescale.

d. In both types of organisation the larger the number and the greater diversity of funders the less real constraint demands for accountability are likely to impose on management.

e. Accountability to government, whether as funder or regulator, may be increasingly important to many for-profit and non-profit organisations.

f. Both types of organisation are under growing pressure to be more accountable to customers, end-users and society in general. For various reasons for-profit organisations may in reality be subject to greater public scrutiny in these respects than non-profit organisations.

1

Introduction

Non-Profit Organisations and Management

Traditionally voluntary organisations have taken little interest in 'management'. Doing good has been seen as sufficient in itself and non-profit organisations have been reluctant to spend money on anything other than the immediate task. But lack of interest goes deeper than that.

'Management' may be not merely unnecessary but positively dangerous. Non-profit organisations may well point out that they have survived and, in many cases, thrived without the benefit of highly paid managers and fancy management theories. Organisations have feared that their goals will be deflected by 'professional' managers and management concepts and practices largely drawn from the for-profit sector. Many non-profit organisations do not accept the tendency to conflate 'businesslike' and 'efficient' with professional management and have yet to be convinced that management concepts and techniques derived from the for-profit sector are the best or the only ones available.

Increasingly, however, non-profit organisations are becoming interested in 'management' and are tending to employ professional managers – often ones trained and with experience in the commercial sector. In part the sector's new-found interest in formal management stems from growth in the size, scope and complexity of its organisations. In total the charity sector alone has an estimated income of over £16 billion per annum and employs around 250,000 people, or 1.5 million if volunteers are taken into account. Many non-profit organisations not only manage large budgets and numbers of staff but also increasingly complex sources of funding and areas of activity.

A second source of the non-profit sector's growing interest in management is related to both its dependence on statutory funding and also the increased competition for other sources of funding. Both, in different ways and for different reasons, demand close attention to efficiency and effectiveness and a more professional and analytical approach to what is done, why and at what cost. Another related pressure stems from closer links with for-profit organisations, especially but not solely, in the form of funding. One consequence of these links may be institutional isomorphism – organisations come to resemble one another. It is certainly true that voluntary non-profit organisations have adopted many of the structures and much of the language of for-profit organisations.

A third and more recent pressure for more 'management' stems from the sector's changing relationship with government and its role in relation to public policy and provision. Recent Conservative governments have emphasised 'partnership' with both the non-profit and for-profit sectors in a wide range of provisions. Contracting-out of public services is now the order of the day. Contracting-out is likely both to increase the size of the sector and of individual organisations and to increase pressures for costing and for greater efficiency and demonstrable effectiveness. Furthermore, contracting-out, combined with continuing pressure on public expenditure, is likely to increase demands for charging consumers for services received from both for-profit and non-profit organisations. These various trends may not only increase, and change, the management needs of non-profit organisations but may also make it evermore difficult to distinguish clearly, in principle and in practice, between non-profit and for-profit organisations.

There are those who acknowledge that non-profit organisations are already, and in future will be increasingly, looking to business schools, management consultants and experienced managers for help in managing the new, larger, more complex non-profit organisations operating under greater public/government scrutiny and in more complex political and funding contexts. Nevertheless, some argue, existing management theory and practice are seriously deficient in meeting the needs of non-profit organisations.

As Mel Moyer, an influential American non-profit management theorist, argues:

> *Historically management scholars have tended to neglect those organizations that are not companies, that are not profit seeking, that are not large, that have high ideological content, that offer services rather than products, and that are led by women. There is one enterprise which combines all these analytically awkward features; and given their cumulative selective perception, management scholars have overlooked it almost entirely. It is the voluntary organization. (Mel Moyer quoted in Mason, 1990, p372).*

But is understanding and meeting the needs of voluntary nonprofit organisations merely a matter of applying existing theories and practices to a somewhat different sort of organisation? Or, as some would argue, are non-profit organisations so fundamentally different from the for-profit organisation, on which management theory and practice are based, that they require a radically different approach? Before examining this question it is worth considering not what, or whether, the non-profit sector has something to learn from (predominantly for-profit) management scholars but what the management scholar has to learn from non-profits.

Why Study the Non-Profit Sector?

Why should management scholars be interested in the voluntary or non-profit sector?

The first answer to this question is the fact that, as noted above, the non-profit sector is growing rapidly in size and employing increasing numbers of managers, many from for-profit organisations (Bruce and Raymer). For this reason alone management scholars may need to take an interest in the sector.

Related to the sector's growth in size is its increasing significance in relation to public policy and provision. Contracting-out is likely to increase further the size of the non-profit sector and to bring the for-profit and non-profit sectors into closer, co-operative and competitive, contact with each other. Thus, the second reason for studying the non-profit sector is that non-profit and for-profit organisations will increasingly find themselves working in collaboration and in competition. If they are to work effectively with or against each other, for-profit and non-profit organisation managers need to understand their similarities and differences.

Thirdly, as organisations from different sectors increasingly work in areas and ways which impinge on each other, they need to understand not merely their similarities and differences but also the philosophical and organisational limits to the effective exchange/convergence of management practices.

Fourthly, study of the non-profit sector provides management scholars with a valuable 'laboratory' for understanding the operation, effects and implications of some management concepts and practices which have been recently 'discovered' by the for-profit sector but which have a long history in the non-profit sector. In addition, the non-profit sector may provide a 'laboratory' for study of the operation of 'old' management theories and practices under different conditions. By studying the voluntary sector management scholars may discover that each sector has something to teach and to learn from the other.

Learning from Each Other

Just as voluntary organisations are discovering commercially dominated management skills, for-profit managers/ theorists are discovering the voluntary sector as one source of ideas for change.

In an article entitled 'The Coming of the New Organization' Drucker argues that in future the typical business will be knowledge-based, composed largely of specialists who direct and discipline their own work through organised feedback from colleagues, customers and headquarters. These organisations will be information-based and will bear little resemblance to the typical manufacturing company, circa 1950, which textbooks still consider the norm. Instead it is far more likely to resemble organizations that neither the practicing manager nor the management scholar pays much attention to today: the hospital, the university, the symphony orchestra. And one might add the non-profit voluntary organisation (Drucker, 1988, p.45).

In a later chapter I shall suggest that many non-profit organisations are indeed predominantly information-based and composed largely of specialists/professionals and volunteers who claim the right to direct and discipline their own performance. For this reason alone management scholars may find it profitable to look more closely at the management characteristics and problems of non-profit organisations as examples of 'organisations of the future'.

Elsewhere Drucker goes so far as to argue that non-profit organisations are worth studying because the best management is found in such organisations (Drucker, 1989).This may be overstating the case but such a view coming from Drucker has to be taken seriously. Certainly if 'best management' is equated with the principles laid down in such popular texts as Peters and Waterman's *In Search of Excellence* then non-profits are worth a closer look (Peters and Waterman, 1982).

Peters and Waterman suggest that eight attributes characterise 'excellent' American commercial companies. These are: a bias for action, staying close to the customer, autonomy and entrepreneurship, productivity through people, a hands-on and value-driven approach, sticking to the knitting, simple form and lean staff, and simultaneous loose-tight properties. These eight attributes might well be a description of the ideology, if not the practice, of many non-profit organisations.

First, many non-profit organisations display a bias for action – for getting on and doing things rather than talking or thinking about it. Indeed, some would argue that this bias is too pronounced and that non-profits display the disadvantages of following this 'rule' too closely. Secondly, non-profits emphasise their concern for the wishes and needs of their customers; this is what in many respects provides them with their raison d'etre. But they also demonstrate the difficulties of putting principle into practice. Thirdly, autonomy and entrepreneurship are an important part of the ideology of the non-profit sector which prides itself on being a source of innovation. But again non-profit organisations experience difficulties in combining autonomy and entrepreneurship with consistency, strategic corporate planning and efficiency.

Fourthly, people are typically seen as the key resource of the non-profit organisation. Many have no other resource and even those with a substantial income are still likely to emphasise the importance of involving staff and volunteers in the work of the organisation. Fifthly, non-profits also stress the importance of a hands-on, value driven approach; values are at the core of the organisation's mission and hands-on knowledge and involvement are considered crucial. Sixthly, for various reasons, non-profits display a strong tendency to 'stick to the knitting' – to stay close to the business they know best although I shall suggest some exceptions below. Seventhly, although it is debatable whether many non-profits could be decribed as displaying a simple form, they are likely to display lean staff. 'Lean staff' may be due to lack of income and/or because a large paid staff and high expenditure on 'administration' are frowned on as an unnecessary diversion of charitable resources.

Finally, many non-profits have simultaneous loose-tight structures, strongly emphasising core values but allowing workers considerable freedom within that. As noted above, the emphasis on core values stems from their centrality to mission and, for some, to charitable status. Core values are the only thing that holds many non-profit organisations together. At the same time, voluntary non-profit organisations arguably have little choice but to allow considerable freedom in the pursuit of core values because apart from the paid staff who are likely to be professionals, the rest are unpaid volunteers whose recruitment and retention may depend on a mixture of values and freedom.

These points will be discussed in more detail in the following chapter. The important point here is that non-profit organisations provide an opportunity to study the supposed attributes of excellence, the gap between ideology and practice and some of the unforeseen consequences of those attributes. Non-profit organisations may not only display the key attributes of 'excellence' but also their sometimes less than excellent implications.

There are other important issues to be addressed in exploring the possibility and limitations of learning and teaching between the sectors. At a theoretical level, the exploration raises issues about the very existence of 'generic management skills' on which much management education is founded. In the United States the non-profit sector's 'discovery' of management has generated a lively debate on whether it is possible to teach generic management or whether the management problems of non-profits are so different that separate skills are required. At a practical level, issues are raised concerning the growing movement of staff from for-profits into non-profits (Bruce and Raymer). Why is this happening and is it appropriate? Could movement also work in the opposite direction (i.e. from non-profits into for-profits)? This movement generates other questions: what do individuals find attractive about non-profits, and could for-profit organisations replicate these attractions in order to keep or better motivate staff?

Thus perhaps the most powerful reason for devoting greater attention to the non-profit sector is that, taken together with the already developed study of management in for-profit organisations, it will provide the basis for a better understanding of the variety of management and a 'testing ground' for analysis of the implications of both old and 'new' practices. By seeking the best and discarding the worst of management practices from both for- and non-profit organisations management thinking and practice may be enlarged and enriched.

Studying the Non-Profit Sector

To suggest that it would be useful to look more closely at non-profit organisations and their management is one thing. To do it is another.

One of the many paradoxes in this area is the fact that, while current policy and practice are leading to increasing integration of the voluntary, statutory and commercial sectors, academic writing and research are increasingly separating off the voluntary/non-profit sector as a distinct area of study. Despite these attempts to carve out a new and supposedly distinctive domain, however, there is still no consensus on how to define or classify non-profit organisations. Non-profits go by various names -the voluntary sector, non-governmental organisations, the independent sector, the third or non-profit sector. Whatever the terminology, the category is usually residual, including any organisation that is not strictly governmental or profit seeking – though sometimes public sector organisations are included. Some definitions substitute 'nonprofit distributing' for non-profit-seeking as a more accurate description of modern non-profits.

In the following chapter I shall look at some characteristics of non-profit organisations. These characteristics are often alleged to make the structure and management of such organisations fundamentally different from those of forprofits, thus suggesting, first, that there is a distinctive non-profit sector and, secondly, that management concepts and practices derived from the for-profit world are of limited value in the non-profit sector. I attempt to disentangle similarities and differences within the non-profit sector, and between the for-profit and non-profit sectors, and the sources of those differences. Attention to sources is important. For example, some differences between for-profit and non-profit organisations stem from charitable status but not all non-profits are charities; other differences may stem from the presence of volunteers but not all non-profits involve volunteers. I shall suggest that on closer examination of the variety of non-profit organisations the supposedly distinctive characteristics of the sector are not so distinctive after all.

Conclusion

Understanding the characteristics of and distinctions between non-profit and for-profit organisations is increasingly important to managers in the public, private and voluntary sectors. A major thrust of current government policy is to encourage partnerships between the sectors, bringing them closer together by applying the standards, language and concepts of for-profit management to all. At the same time, however, there is increasing disenchantment with the values and practices of for-profit organisations. Furthermore, many for-profit organisations are discovering precisely those attributes and ways of working which have traditionally been associated with the voluntary sector. At present, most of the knowledge and manpower goes one way from for-profits to non-profits, but the tide may be turning and the future may produce something closer to a two-way traffic. But do we really understand enough about either sector to be able to distinguish what is worth having and what should be left to die? Will the for-profit sector steal the non-profits' best clothes while giving something less good in return? Are the voluntary sector clothes really worth having? If *In Search of Excellence* had been researched in the voluntary sector would it have found that many of the principles on which excellence is supposedly based do not always work or have other less attractive side-effects?

Answers to these questions are urgently needed if both non-profit and for-profit organisations are to avoid costly diversions and mistakes. The answers will certainly not be simple and will equally certainly require a willingness to dispense with established stereotypes and divisions in order to examine similarities and differences both within and between sectors. This paper is not a discussion of the differences between the for-profit and non-profit sectors; rather it attempts to identify similarities and differences between organisations within and across the sectors.

2
The Variety of Non-Profit Organisations

Before considering the structural and management differences between non-profit and for-profit organisations it is clearly important to look at the variety of organisations within the non-profit sector.

For many people non-profit organisations are synonymous with charities, but not all non-profit organisations are charities and charities are a very mixed and somewhat surprising bag. If the mythical man in the street were asked to say which of the following – Oxfam, Age Concern, the Medical Research Council, Eton, Amnesty International, the Arts Council, Save the Children Fund – is not a charity he would probably plump for Eton, the Medical Research Council or the Arts Council. In fact, the only organisation in the list above which is not a charity is Amnesty International.

Non-profit organisations are part of the charity sector, the non-profit sector, the voluntary sector, the independent sector, the third sector and so on. These different terms reflect attempts to get round the fact that non-profit organisations are not necessarily charities, nor necessarily voluntary in the sense of involving volunteers or in the sense of relying upon voluntary donations, nor are they necessarily independent in the sense of being independent of government funding. They are not even non-profit insofar as many earn, even if they do not distribute, surpluses.

The non-profit sector is most usually recognised by what it is not – it is not profit-seeking and it is not straighforwardly part of the public sector (although some definitions do include some public sector organisations). The non-profit sector is thus a residual category containing all those organisations which do not clearly fit into either the commercial for-profit sector or the public sector.

There are very real questions to be asked about whether this residual category has any analytical worth; is it useful to lump together in one category organisations which may have little in common except that they are not something else? Do these organisations have anything distinctive in common or are we misleading ourselves in thinking that they do simply because they all belong to this residual category?

In this chapter I shall first look at the range of organisations included within the non-profit sector and then discuss some ways in which different types of organisation might be identified. The final section considers growth and change in such organisations and the way in which organisations may change type. This chapter provides the basis for later discussion of the similarities and differences within and between the for-profit and non-profit sectors, focusing in particular on management structures, tasks and constraints.

The Range of Non-Profit Organisations

No-one knows how many organisations in Britain fit into the non-profit category. We do know, however, that there were over 166,000 registered charities at the end of 1991, and that new charities are being added at the rate of around 4,000 per annum, while only around 1,000 per annum are removed from the register. Although charitable registration is not an option for all non-profits (for reasons discussed below), the tax advantages of charitable status are such that all non-profits which qualify for registration are likely to seek it. Thus charities may form the bulk of non-profit organisations.

The activities covered by non-profits include provision of higher education, private education, medical research, various welfare services, animal welfare, environmental campaigns and so on. Organisations vary in style from the small self-help group to the large welfare bureaucracies as well as the small and large campaigning organisations. They may be purely local or international in scope.

Charities. The best data on the sector concern charities, which are estimated to have a total annual income of around £16 billion Around £1 billion of this comes in government grants and over £8 billion from fees and charges (which include fees paid by local and central government for services provided). These figures alone illustrate that the sector is neither independent of government nor unfamiliar with 'trading'. Total staff employed by charities are estimated at around 250,000, or 1.5 million if volunteers are included — illustrating that even charities are by no means synonymous with volunteer organisations.

But these aggregate data conceal significant differences within the sector. Even within the narrow category of registered charities there are major differences in size, sources of income, age and origins.

Size. The vast majority of charities have very low incomes, no paid staff and only a handful of volunteers/members. A survey of the distribution of charitable income in 1975 revealed that the top 5% of charities commanded 83% of the total income (Austin and Posnett, 1979). In terms of numbers the big household names constitute a tiny minority of all charities but they consume the great majority of charity income, employ the majority of staff and involve the majority of volunteers. For example, in 1986 the National Trust had an income of £68 million, involved thousands of volunteers, had 1.5 million members and employed 2,000 staff. Many charities, universities for example, are much bigger than this.

Sources of Income. In 1990 Oxfam had a total income of over £62 million of which over £45m came from voluntary sources, almost £6m from government grants and over £3.5m from trading. The National Trust in the same year had a total income of £104m, with over £55m from voluntary sources, around £13m from trading and sale of goods and services and around £6m from government (CAF 1991). Age Concern England, with an income of over £10.5m in 1990 derived almost half of its income from government sources and almost half from voluntary sources. By contrast, the Wellcome Trust, with a total income of £63m in 1990, did no fund-raising and received no government grants deriving its entire income from its very considerable assets (£3,250m in 1990). Some charities — the Medical Research Council, the Arts Council, and the Independent Living Fund, for example — are almost entirely funded by government, whereas most public/private schools (also charities) derive the vast majority of their income from fees and charges. Other charities — large and small — are solely, or very heavily, dependent upon fund-raising from corporate and individual donors.

Age and origins. Some charities are very old, others are relatively or very new. As noted above, increase in charity registrations is currently running at around 4,000 per annum. Whereas many of the older charities have religious origins most of the new ones are likely to be secular. Many new charities are also the creation not of altruistic individuals but directly or indirectly of local and central government. This growth in government-'inspired', and often wholly funded, charities has been noted in Britain and in the United States and forms part of what Salamon has referred to as 'third party government' in which government uses third parties to pursue its policy goals (Salamon, 1987). This trend, likely to accelerate in Britain in the coming years as a direct result of the policies of recent Conservative governments, has obvious and important implications for management and control in charities and non-profit organisations. Even those charities which were originally 'private' independent bodies may become agents of government policy via their increasing dependence upon government funding; again this trend looks set to accelerate with the growth of contracting-out service provision from the public to the voluntary/non-profit sector.

Legal Structures

In addition to the above differences, the broad category of voluntary non-profit organisations conceals important differences in legal status and requirements. Not all non-profits are charities enjoying the tax advantages of such status, nor are they subject to the restrictions on political activity and trading which this status brings. Charitable status is also important insofar as it imposes restrictions on the management structure of the organisation. All registered charities must have charity trustees, who are debarred from enjoying any personal gain from the charity. This means that they cannot be paid for the work they do and cannot be employed by the organisation, which in turn means that paid staff cannot sit on the trustee body. One way round this restriction, adopted by some charities, is to have a separate management committee on which paid staff are allowed to sit. But, as Adirondack (1989) points out:

> The trustees have ultimate responsibility for a charity, which can cause problems if the trustees and the management committee do not know what each other is doing or disagree about what the organisation should do (p.14).

Further or similar complications may arise if the charity is also a limited company with company directors who are different from the trustees.

All of these differences have obvious implications for those wishing to make statements about the non-profit sector as a whole and to compare management in the non-profit and for-profit sectors. Managing five people is very different from managing 500. Managing a volunteer-dominated organisation with hundreds of very part-time volunteers without money/pay as a carrot or a stick, is different from managing a large or small organisation entirely composed of paid professional staff. Managing an organisation entirely dependent upon inherently uncertain and variable income from donations by the general public is different from managing one largely dependent upon government funding. Managing service provision is different from managing campaigning or from managing a democratic selfhelp group in which even to talk of management may be anathema. Generalisations about the characteristics and management needs of non-profit organisations are as inappropriate as those which treat all for-profit organisations as though they were fundamentally the same.

Types of Non-Profit Organisation

Given the variety concealed within the category of the 'nonprofit sector', is it possible to distinguish broad types of non-profit organisations about which valid generalisations, and comparisons with for-profit organisations, might be made?

Considerable effort has been expended on this task over the years without any very satisfactory results. The problem is partly that typologies are useful for different purposes; how satisfactory a given set of distinctions is depends very much on what one wants to use it for. The other difficulty in finding a truly satisfactory typology of non-profit organisations lies in the fact that in practice such organisations tend to elude neat categorisation, always irritatingly straddling the boundaries. It is, however, worth spending some time looking at the available typologies because, whether or not they are applicable in practice to any one organisation, they do highlight some of the key characteristics of non-profit organisations, as well as some distinctions useful in understanding different organisational and thus management characteristics and tasks.

Categorisation by industry. Some classifications of non-profit organisations distinguish in terms of major purpose or area of activity, much as one might distinguish in the for-profit sector between different industries (see, for example, Knapp and Kendal, 1991).

Categorisation by source of income. Some writers have suggested that the key difference among non-profit organisations and one which affects how they operate, is source of income and/or independence from government. So, for example, Mullin (1980) distinguishes among non-profits in terms of dependence on government. But one might equally well distinguish among organisations in terms of their dependence on, and the conditions attached to, any major source of income on the assumption that dependence on any single income/market makes a difference to management and operation.

The distinction among non-profits in terms of their independence of government is often discussed in the non-profit sector and it is interesting to consider whether it has any equivalent in the analysis of for-profit organisations. In other words, is any single/heavy dependency upon one source of income considered a major relevant criterion in understanding differences among for-profit organisations? Certainly some analysts have considered it useful in understanding structures of control to distinguish among for-profit organisations in terms of the composition/distribution of shareholders; and for-profit organisations themselves may devote considerable energy to expanding their markets thus avoiding over-dependence upon any particular segment/source of income. Clearly, however, an organisation's relationship to its funding source(s) is only one aspect in understanding what makes it work and the constraints under which it must operate.

Bases of participation. Some of the earliest attempts to distinguish among non-profit organisations arose from a more general interest in organisations, their variety and their management. So, for example, Clark and Wilson, clearly influenced by Chester Barnard's pioneering work on organisation and management, distinguish among organisations in terms of the incentives offered to individuals to contribute to the group/organisation. Distinguishing among material, solidary and purposive incentives, Clark and Wilson (1961) suggest that voluntary/non-profit organisations differ from other types of organisation in their reliance on solidary incentives such as sociability, fun and prestige.

Clark and Wilson's typology is now somewhat outdated in that voluntary organisations increasingly offer material incentives. But it may still have its uses in distinguishing among organisations. The extent to which managers can rely on material incentives to motivate staff or need to provide other incentives for participation and satisfaction may constitute an important difference among organisations and is a theme which is touched on in other typologies outlined below.

Who benefits? Blau and Scott's typology of organisations is based not on why people contribute but on who benefits. Thus, in mutual benefit organisations the prime beneficiary is the membership; in service organisations it is the client; in 'commonwealth' organisations it is the public at large; and in business organisations it is the owners (Blau and Scott, 1962).

Mission. Another set of typologies is based on the purposes/mission of the organisation. So, for example, Rose suggested that there are only two types of non-profit/voluntary association – expressive groups and social influence associations. Expressive groups act to express or satisfy interests which the members have in relation to themselves, and would include sports associations, scientific associations and so on. Social influence associations concentrate their efforts on the society in order to bring about some desired condition or change (Rose, 1967).

Though somewhat crude and oversimplified, this distinction in terms of mission highlights a fundamental difference between organisations in the extent to which they look 'out' or 'in', and in that sense has obvious management implications. However, a more useful distinction is probably that between expressive and instrumental organisations. Expressive organisations exist primarily to express or satisfy members' interests, whereas instrumental organisations aim to get things done usually for/with others. The goals of expressive organisations lie inside the group, whereas those of instrumental organisations lie outside.

Gordon and Babchuk develop this typology by distinguishing between expressive, instrumental and instrumental-expressive non-profit organisations. They recognise that the dichotomy of expressive and instrumental organisations is an oversimplification in that many organisations seem to have both functions. For example, a voluntary organisation may have an instrumental mission and be organised accordingly at the national level, but in its local fund-raising branches it may serve a primarily expressive function operating as a social club for members. They also recognise that even organisations which are primarily instrumental in the definition of their goals as lying outside the organisation itself may nevertheless serve expressive functions for their staff (Gordon and Babchuk, 1959). Indeed, much of modern for-profit management theory implies that one of the marks of a successful/'excellent' for-profit instrumental organisation is that it creates expressive satisfactions for staff in fulfilling its instrumental goals (see, for example, Peters and Waterman, 1982).

Accessibility and status. Gordon and Babchuk suggest that voluntary organisations are differentiated not only by the character of their goals but also by their degree of accessibility and by their status-conferring capacity. Degree of accessibility refers to the conditions for membership/involvement; anyone can join some organisations but others require certain characteristics (for example, being a woman or having certain types of experience or a university degree or professional qualification). Status-conferring capacity refers to the

> capacity of an organisation to bestow prestige or to be associated with prestige which accrues to its members' (Gordon and Babchuk, 1959).

These three variables – type of goal/mission, status conferring and accessibility – provide 12 types of voluntary organisation. Although Gordon and Babchuk are not primarily concerned with the implications for management, it is likely that the organisation's place in the typology will affect the management task. For example, it will, by definition, be easier to attract participants in organisations with high accessibility; but if the organisation also has instrumental goals this may create management difficulties insofar as some of those to whom the organisation is accessible may not be best suited/qualified to achieve these goals (see below for further discussion of this point).

Problems in 'placing' organisations. Gordon and Babchuk allude to, but do not develop, one crucial distinction in considering any typology of organisations – that between what the organisation is in theory about and how the participants perceive what it is about or what in practice they seek from it. For example, the Board, the director and paid staff may clearly see the organisation as instrumental or purposive – the organisation exists to get things done in the 'outside' world. But the volunteers may see it is as solidary or expressive: the organisation exists to fulfil their needs. Managers ignore these differences at their peril.

The second important point in considering where an organisation fits in any typology is that organisations do not stand still. In particular, they may change over time from being primarily expressive to being primarily instrumental and this change may bring its own management problems, not least that of reconciling the perceptions of participants with the new mission of the organisation. Before exploring this point further it is important to note two other important variables in understanding non-profit organisations and their management structures.

First, non-profit, like for-profit, organisations vary in the levels at which they operate. Some are purely local, others purely national, others operate at both levels. Secondly, organisations vary in the relationship between levels. Again, it is important to recognise that there may be differences in perceptions and demands between levels. For example, an organisation operating nationally may adopt a corporate style with little difficulty but if an organisation operating at both national and local levels does so it may encounter difficulties if its local 'branches' perceive this as an encroachment on what they see as a federal relationship with the national body. Similarly, difficulties may arise if the headquarters national body sees the organisation's purpose as instrumental, while the local branches see it as expressive or solidary.

The above discussion highlights two important points. First, non-profit organisations are not all the same and they vary in ways which may fundamentally affect management structures, tasks and needs. Secondly, non-profit organisations may display different characteristics at different levels or in different parts of the organisation and, in addition, the characteristics and structure of an organisation may change over time.

Changing Types. No organisation stands still. Its mission/purposes and structure change as the organisation ages and grows – or contracts – and in relation to changes in the external environment.

One of the simplest but for many purposes most useful typologies of voluntary/non-profit organisations is that developed by Charles Handy. The typology not only distinguishes among types of organisation but also has built into it a theory of change. Handy's typology combines many of the variables discussed above – who benefits, accessibility of participation, instrumental versus expressive goals, and so on – in especially illuminating ways.

Handy distinguishes three types of organisation: Mutual support organisations are 'Those organisations which are created in order to put people with a particular problem or enthusiasm in touch with others like themselves who can give them understanding, advice, support and encouragement' (Handy, 1981, p.13). This is how many voluntary organisations start.

Service delivery organisations are instrumental organisations 'in the business of providing services to those in need'. Typically they employ large numbers of paid staff.

Campaigning organisations are organisations created to campaign for a cause or to act as a pressure group for a particular interest.

Each of these types, Handy argues, carries with it an unspoken assumption about the nature of the organisation and how it ought to be managed.

Mutual aid groups need only the minimum amount of organisation to service the members, to find reasons for meetings and to publicise themselves. Anyone who is interested can join and 'No one is going to vet them for intelligence, analyse their job record or give them an aptitude test'. Mutual aid groups do not want to be managed and regard administration as a distraction; at most they want to be serviced.

Service delivery organisations are quite different. They are instrumental and are all about organisation to get the job done:

> *They take pride in being professional, effective and lowcost. It follows that they need to be selective about their recruits, demanding in their review of standards, prepared to reprimand where necessary, even to dismiss someone whose work is inadequate (p.14).*

You cannot by choice join the core of this type of organisation. These organisations tend to be bureaucratic in the sense that jobs have formal definitions with formal responsibilities and formal accountability; the organisation needs to be able to continue operating in the same way even if individuals move on.

Campaigning organisations are led rather than managed. They need administration but this is subordinate and preferably invisible:

> *The essence of the organisation is that of adherence to a cause, focused on a leader, often a charismatic one whose personality infects the organisation. The only qualification for belonging is that you believe, and the more believers the better (p.14).*

Each set of assumptions hangs together and there are different ways of organising for each set. But what tends to happen is that a mutual aid organisation moves over time into service delivery or a service delivery organisation begins to campaign 'the logic is clear but the clash of assumptions can be heard from miles away ' (Handy, 1988).

In the same vein Rowe suggests a move from self-help to altruistic organisations (expressive to instrumental, mutual support to service delivery) with corresponding changes in organisational structure. He raises important questions about the effects of this move on voluntary organisations' supposedly 'participative' character, their involvement of members and users in key decisions, their ability to respond effectively to consumers and their accountability (Rowe, 1978). These issues will be dealt with in subsequent chapters of this paper.

Change Factors and Processes

Much of the work on change in non-profit organisations is less concerned with types of organisation and more concerned with the ways in which change occurs and what it does to the organisation.

Many studies of change factors and processes in non-profit organisations are based on organisation theory applicable to all organisations whether for-profit or non-profit. Arguably, however, there are special problems with change in non-profits because, as we have seen, change may lead to different parts of the organisation becoming 'out of step'. For example, the staff and Board may see the need for the organisation to become less accessible in order to pursue instrumental goals/deliver services more efficiently – but existing volunteers may resist this change. Of course, similar problems may emerge in for-profit organisations. But, it may be argued, these problems are more threatening to voluntary organisations because the latter are more likely to be dependent upon volunteers for survival and legitimacy and because they do not have the incentive of pay to hold people; volunteers and members really can take it or leave it. Another argument is that for-profit organisations can change their goals within an overall mission of profit maximisation; but because the substantive mission is central to its raison d'etre, a non-profit organisation cannot so easily adapt to change without self-destructing.

Powell and Friedkin identify three broad approaches to organisational change which are applicable to all organisations in whatever sector (Powell and Friedkin, 1989). The first approach sees organisational change as a reaction to internal conditions. So, for example, change in the for-profit sector from a functional to a multi-divisional form has been explained as a consequence of the internal need to co-ordinate and manage large-scale growth and expansion. Other studies have stressed the tendency in all organisations for operational goals to supplant purposive ones. In other words, the activities of the organisation become centred around the proper functioning of procedures rather than upon the achievement of the goals the organisation exists to achieve (Selznick, 1975). Michels' 'iron law of oligarchy' comes into this category of explanation of change (Michels, 1962). In order to retain their high status positions in the organisation participants put more energy into self-serving activities than into goal-directed ones. Non-profit organisations, Powell and Friedkin suggest, are particularly vulnerable to this 'law', not least because of the growth of professionalisation in such organisations and because, with a large and only semi-involved rank and file, leaders may come to feel that they are the only people who really understand the organisation.

The second approach to explaining change emphasises the tendency of organisations to alter their structures and goals in order to obtain the resources needed to survive. This resource-dependence approach suggests, for example, that non-profit organisations will adapt their structures and goals to those of government bodies to the extent that they need or become dependent upon such sources of funding.

The third approach explains change as a result of institutional isomorphism (DiMaggio and Powell, 1983). Briefly, this approach posits the existence of 'organisational fields' made up of key suppliers, resource and product consumers, regulatory agencies and other organisations that produce similar services and products. Through increased interaction, exchange of information, the development of structures of prestige and of an 'institutionalised mind-set', organisations in the same field alter their structures and behaviour to conform to the norms of the field. So, for example, there are those who would argue that non-profit organisations are becoming more and more like local authority social services departments as they interact with them in the contracting-out process, taking on local authority goals and values, structures and processes to facilitate this process and gain approval. Similar points have been made about the effects of corporate giving to non-profit organisations: recipient organisations adopt the behaviour, structures and processes which corporate donors consider acceptable and in which they have confidence. As Powell and Friedkin acknowledge, it is sometimes difficult to disentangle the effects of resource-dependence from those of institutional isomorphism.

Conclusion

This chapter has illustrated the variety and complexity within the non-profit sector and reviewed some ways in which analysts have attempted to deal with this variety by distinguishing types of organisation within the voluntary/non-profit sector. There is no 'typical' non-profit organisation, just as there is no typical for-profit organisation. For that reason alone generalisations about the non-profit sector and comparisons between non-profit and for-profit organisations must be made with great caution. Similarly, recognition of organisational variety must underlie all analyses of management structures and needs in non-profit organisations.

Non-profit organisations are not only different from each other but any one organisation may change. Arguably, the pace and direction of change in non-profit organisations may themselves be changing. The tendency of non-profits to become more instrumental and more service-oriented, to emphasise standards and evaluation, to employ more paid staff, to become more bureaucratic as they grow is reinforced in the current policy context which stresses 'partnerships' with both the statutory and for-profit sectors.

Non-profits, through the processes of resource-dependence and institutional isomorphism, are becoming more like their public and private sector 'colleagues' in a whole range of ways from increased trading to adoption of professional management structures and processes. As noted above, at the same time for-profit organisations are also changing, not least in their discovery of the importance of solidary, expressive characteristics in successful organisations. For-profit organisations are increasingly recognised as places where people live out their lives fulfilling needs to be creative, to gain esteem and to exercise responsibility. Many for-profit organisations are acknowledging that they need to be more than instrumental machines if they are to work most effectively. The net result of these two trends may be increasing convergence between non-profit and for-profit organisations. Or are the differences more fundamental?

3
Managing without Profit

Following the discussion of the complex variety of non-profit organisations, this chapter considers a characteristic of non-profits which in theory is possessed by all such organisations and which, again in theory, clearly distinguishes them from for-profit organisations. The literature on non-profit management assigns a central place to the fact that non-profit organisations manage without profit, without a clear quantitative bottom-line. Many of the supposedly distinctive features and difficulties of non-profit management are attributed to this one defining characteristic. Before looking at some of the management problems created by lack of profit, it is worth making two fundamental points.

The first point is that many non-profit organisations do make profits or surpluses in particular areas of activity. What is supposedly distinctive about non-profits is that they do not distribute these profits. Whereas it is true that at some periods in their existence some for-profit organisations do not distribute profits, the lack of profit distribution is a temporary measure requiring explanation, whereas in the non-profit organisation it is supposedly a defining characteristic – even if 'the rewards offered to senior staff in the most competitive voluntary organnisations raise questions even about this distinction' (Taylor, 1991, p.66).

The second point concerns profit as a goal. The notion that profit is a simple and straightforward concept in commercial organisations is far from the truth. Even among for-profit organisations there are arguments about the significance which should be attributed to profit as opposed to other financial measures, about what counts as profit and over what timescale it should be measured. Different types of firms with different management control in differently structured markets may see the significance and measurement of profit somewhat differently. So, for example, it has been suggested that the timescale over which profit is measured will be shorter for smaller firms operating in precarious markets; larger firms in more stable markets tend to have longer profit horizons.

Apart from differences in timescales, firms may differ in the significance attached to profit maximisation as a key goal. Thus both Baumol and Williamson have suggested that in manager-controlled firms growth of sales revenue is likely to be an equally if not more important objective. For various reasons sales-revenue maximisation gives the manager greater control and greater status (Baumol, 1959; Williamson, 1963). Marris has argued that the goal which both owners and managers share is not profit maximisation *per se*, nor sales revenue, but growth (Marris, 1964). A major study by Shipley of 728 UK firms concluded that only 15.9% of them could be regarded as profit maximisers. However, 88% of firms included it as part of their set of goals (Shipley, 1981). The modern theory of corporations recognises that the firm is a coalition of participants with disparate demands. Insofar as profit is necessary for survival the profit objective will be shared by all, but the appropriate level of profit needed for survival may be subject to dispute.

It may also be important to distinguish between overall profit and profit in relation to particular segments or products. Various studies show that firms engage in portfolio planning such that profitable products provide the funds to raise new products to maturity (Haspeslaugh, 1982; Sizer, 1982). Thus, firms which engage in portfolio planning may tolerate lack of profit on a particular line in much the same way as non-profit organisations cover the deficit on some services with income from other sources.

As I shall suggest below, lack of profit as a bottom-line does create difficulties in establishing performance indicators in non-profit organisations, but it is important to remember that the measurement of profit is itself problematic and is not, in any case, the only basis for establishing performance indicators in for-profit organisations.

What are the implications of managing without profit creation and distribution as a key organisational characteristic?

Capitalisation and Revenue Sources

Various writers have pointed to the fact that one of the major disadvantages faced by non-profit organisations, arising from their lack of profit distribution, is that they are limited in their ability to raise capital (Hansmann, 1981). When voluntary organisations are able to raise capital from commercial sources it is likely to be strictly tied to their assets rather than related to notions of future prospects. On the other hand, voluntary organisations may be able to raise capital from charitable trusts and foundations. Such capital is likely to be a gift rather than a loan and to require no security other than that provided by the organisation's reputation and demonstrated competence.

The difference between for-profit and non-profit organisations in their ability to raise capital may lie not solely in the availability of capital but also in the conditions attached to capital acquisition. Arguably, however, voluntary organisations may be in much the same position as some small businesses. One of the greatest difficulties of both non-profit and for-profit organisations in their early years is ensuring sufficient capitalisation. Neither is able to borrow from commercial sources much beyond its assets, and both are dependent upon the goodwill – whim – of banks and other lenders.

But there may also be differences. Unlike small businesses, voluntary organisations also have at least the hope of no-interest, non-repayable capital injections in the form of grants from charitable foundations. However, such grants are both limited in number and size and are not equally available to all. Larger, better established organisations with a national reputation and demonstrated competence are likely to be able to raise more capital via this route than smaller, lesser known organisations. It might be argued that the same could be said of lending by commercial organisations – those who already have are able to raise more. The difference, however, is that in commercial lending decisions tangible assets, as well as judgements about future performance, play a key role whereas in grant-making decisions tangible assets are of little or no importance and may actually count against the applicant. In grantmaking decisions reputation and perceived past performance based largely on size of budget rather than tangible, demonstrated results are more important. Thus for the voluntary organisation hoping to raise capital via grants reputation, rather than assets, is crucial; image management is one of the organisation's greatest assets. I shall return to this point below.

One of the major differences between for-profit and non-profit organisations in relation to their need for both capital and revenue funding may be most apparent in recession. In a recession the for-profit organisation experiences a reduction in demand for its services and a corresponding reduction in revenue and in the immediate need for capital expansion. The non-profit organisation, by contrast, is likely to face an *increase* in demand for its services and a correspondingly increased need for capital expansion. But, at the same time, recession is likely to bring reduced revenue funding as well as less ready, or more expensive, access to capital borrowing. To an extent, and for different reasons, some for-profit organisations heavily dependent upon loans may face similar counter-cyclical problems insofar as revenues decrease but demand on those revenues increases due to higher interest rates.

Before leaving the issue of capitalisation it is worth noting that managing without profit does not imply managing without financial risk. As Young has noted, all for-profit ventures involve financial risk, but risk is not unique to for-profit organisations. Furthermore, the financial liability of for-profit entrepreneurs is likely to be hedged by financial institutions whereas in non-profit organisations the risk may be just as real but less well insured (Young, 1987). One difference between the financial risks in the two sectors, however, may be that failure in the for-profit sector is both more obvious and more acceptable, whereas in the non-profit sector it is both less easy to detect and less acceptable.

No Profit, No Performance Indicators?

It is widely accepted in the literature that lack of profit creates significant management difficulties in voluntary organisations insofar as it deprives the organisation of any basis for the establishment of performance indicators. Without profit as a bottom-line, how does the organisation define and recognise success and failure for the organisation as a whole and for individual members of staff?

Certain provisos were noted above regarding profit as the ultimate performance indicator in commercial organisations. But even leaving these aside, it is clear that managing without profit to provide the basis for performance indicators is not peculiar to non-profit organisations. Staff/service departments within for-profit organisations experience similar problems. How do you measure the performance and contribution of information or library departments in a for-profit organisation producing soap-powder?

Others may argue that the real difference between for-profit and non-profit organisations in establishing performance indicators lies not so much in the lack of profit but rather in the intangible nature of what is typically provided by nonprofit organisations.

Moss Kanter and Summers, noting that the measurement of performance is not easy in any organisation, suggest that profit is treated as central in for-profit organisations because it can be measured easily and because it is a good test of market satisfaction and of the capacity of the organisation to run itself efficiently. Non-profit organisations, on the other hand, define themselves not around their financial returns but rather around the services they offer. These services are intangible and difficult to measure and clients, professionals and donors/funders may make different judgements regarding their quality. Thus Moss Kanter and Summers argue that it is not lack of profit *per se* but rather the centrality of (intangible) social values over (objective) financial values that complicates management for non-profit organisations (Moss Kanter and Summers, 1987).

Lack of profit as a bottom line may be a less significant difference than is sometimes assumed between non-profit and for-profit organisations in establishing performance indicators. But inability to *distribute* profit may be an important constraint in some non-profit organisations. Even if performance indicators/measurement can be devised and performance can be measured, the available mechanisms for introducing performance-related pay may be limited by lack of access to benefits such as stock options and profit-sharing plans as well as a fear of accumulating surplus funds which look like profit (Young, 1987).

No Profit, No Competition?

One of the supposed characteristics of the for-profit sector is that it is inherently competitive. Companies vie with each other for customers, for market position and penetration, and ultimately for profit. The non-profit sector, on the other hand, is supposedly characterised by co-operation.

The reality in both sectors is, however, rather different. In the for-profit sector there are monopolies and oligopolies and, in addition, companies may co-operate with each other to protect or further their common interests. Indeed, Moss Kanter sees such co-operation between for-profit companies as one important characteristic of for-profit management in the future (Moss Kanter, 1989). On the other hand, in the non-profit sector bitter rivalries may exist between organisations. Some non-profit organisations exist as a direct comment on the supposed inadequacy of others working in the same or a similar field; and non-profit organisations may compete with each other for public and government support, for funds, for members, volunteers and users and for credibility and legitimacy. The new contractual basis for public funding of many non-profit organisations may heighten this competition and organisations may increasingly evolve strategies to establish dominance in particular market niches (Wilson, 1989; Saxon-Harrold, 1990; Butler and Wilson, 1990).

Competition in the non-profit sector is, however, complicated by several factors. First, some organisations may be wary of the effects of overt competition which challenges the public perception of charities, in particular. Charities are supposed to be dedicated to the pursuit of public benefit rather than bent on organisational dominance; charities are presumed to be devoted to higher ends and to be charitable towards each other. Secondly, in the non-profit sector hostile take-overs are virtually impossible and even friendly mergers generally require permission from the Charity Commission. But thirdly, and perhaps especially interesting, what in the for-profit sector would be regarded as healthy competition promoting choice for consumers is frequently frowned on in the non-profit sector as wasteful duplication. To avoid charges of wasteful duplication some non-profits must therefore be at least as concerned as any for-profit organisation with carving out a distinctive market niche for themselves. Unless they can convince potential supporters that they are different from other apparently similar organisations their survival may be in jeopardy.

4

The Separation of Funder and Consumer

Closely related to managing without profit, the separation of funders and consumers is often regarded as a key characteristic of non-profit organisations. Unlike the situation in for-profit trading organisations, so the argument goes, in non-profit organisations service delivery (output) is separated from resource acquisition (input). This, it is alleged, has various implications, including the need for the organisation to 'face two ways' – to funders and to consumers (Paton and Cornforth, 1992). Furthermore, the non-profit organisation supposedly has a different relationship with its consumers from that of the for-profit trading organisation with its customers (for example, the non-profit organisation usually aims to ration rather than stimulate demand from consumers). There are, however, various problems with this characterisation of resource acquisition in non-profits and with the validity of the contrast with for-profit organisations.

One problem is that funders and consumers are not separated in all voluntary organisations or in all parts of any one organisation. Different types of voluntary organisation and different activities within organisations recover varying amounts of their costs from the end-user/consumer. So, for example, conferences and training events run by non-profit organisations may be designed to fund themselves from charges to participants/consumers and there is increasing pressure on many non-profits in Britain to consider all activities with a view to covering costs via charges imposed on consumers. In addition, as I shall discuss below, contracting by local and central government turns funders giving grants into customers buying services.

But for many voluntary organisations in much of their work end-users/consumers are currently different from funders. What implications does this have for the management of non-profit organisations?

The separation of those who support the agency from the individual consumer who gets or wants the service means that whether the consumer 'gets something for nothing or nothing for nothing is information for which no direct channels of communicaton are provided' (Stanton, 1970). To achieve its goals the voluntary organisation must serve the consumer but to survive it only needs to please the donor/funder. In theory, by controlling negative feedback, the organisation can substitute packaging for product, 'image manipulation may be substituted for direct action.' (Ibid). Of course, for-profit organisations also devote considerable energy to image management in order to seduce customer-funders; but these funders and customers are one and the same, and, therefore, if the product falls too short of the claims made for it image manipulation cannot keep customers. In non-profit organisations image is all, Stanton argues, because the separation of funder and consumer means that funders who are not consumers are not in a position to judge the real quality of the product.

The separation of funder and consumer also means that nonprofit organisations may go on producing goods and services which are increasingly irrelevant to consumers but which funders/donors, through ignorance or because of different values and purposes, are happy to go on funding.

It is undoubtedly true that, when funders and consumers are separated, image management acquires added significance. Image creation is important to voluntary non-profit organisations in persuading donors to give, and in statutory non-profit organisations in legitimating levels of taxation. But image management may also be important to for-profit organisations in raising loans and rights issues. In other words, Stanton's points regarding the separation of funders and consumers and the availability of channels of communication between them do not apply only to voluntary non-profit organisations. Again, we need to look across sectoral boundaries at different types of organisation with different relationships between funders and consumers. In analysing differences between organisations across sectors it may be useful to distinguish between situations in which (i) the user and funder are separate and know little or nothing about each other, (ii) the user and funder are different but are in close contact through, for example, regular meetings or monitoring, and (iii) the funder and user are one and the same.

Drucker puts forward a rather different argument. He attributes fundamental management difficulties to the separation of funder and consumer characteristic of what he calls the public service institution. Public service organisations are paid for their efforts, rather than their results, out of funds someone else has earned. The more effort a public service organisation engages in, the greater its budget will be, and the size of its budget rather than its results are the way in which such organisations define success. It follows from this that any reduction, completion or hiving-off of efforts/activities reduces the success of a public service institution. Public service institutions cannot acknowledge failure if this means loss of a project, and "Worse still the fact that an objective has been attained cannot be admitted" because this too would imply loss of activity and therefore revenue/budget. As a result public service institutions have a built-in resistance to change (Drucker, 1985).

Drucker's analysis relates to all service organisations which are paid for efforts and not for results and out of money someone else has earned. One obvious problem with Drucker's analysis of the funding of public service/non-profit organisations is that it could also apply to departments within for-profit organisations. To what extent do for-profit advertising, public relations or research and development departments define their success by the size of their budget rather than by their results? And to what extent are they paid for efforts rather than results? More generally, Drucker's analysis does not do justice to the complex reality in voluntary, statutory and for-profit organisations.

In considering both Stanton's and Drucker's points it is important to distinguish between organisations, within both the non-profit and for-profit sectors, on the basis of dependence on funding by consumers. In relation to which products/services, and to what extent, is the organisation funded out of charges to consumers? Or, to put it another way, in relation to which products/services, and to what extent, are consumers and funders separated?

Raising income from charges to end-users happens in both sectors. Furthermore, as noted above, there are degrees of separation of funders and end-users. So, for example, both voluntary and statutory non-profit organisations raise income from fees and charges to end-users. Other non-profit activities raise income from funder-customers who meet regularly with end-users. Yet others raise income from funders/donors who have no contact with end-users.

But reality is further complicated by the source of income which does not come from end-users. Thus it may be worth distinguishing between public organisations funded from a budget raised from taxation and organisations whose budget depends on their own fund-raising efforts. Whereas the former must persuade politicians to vote their budgets out of money someone else has earned, the latter must persuade a variety of donors. These donors may include politicians spending money someone else has earned, raised via taxation, as well as corporate and individual donors spending money they themselves have earned and are not required (as in taxation) to give away. Given that donors are people who must be persuaded to part with their money in return for/in recognition of the organisation's 'product' it might be argued that donors are customers and that therefore in this respect customers and funders are not separated. An objection to this argument might be that it simply serves to demonstrate that non-profit organisations have several rather different types of customer. In this respect, I shall suggest below, they are no different from many for-profit organisations.

The separation of customer and funder, supposedly characteristic of public service and voluntary non-profit organisations, may also occur in different ways and to different degrees in the for-profit sector. Indeed, the notion that funder and consumer are always one and the same in for-profit organisations is to adopt a grossly over-simplified, old-fashioned view of the complexities of modern business financing. Leaving aside the difficulty of defining 'customer' and 'consumer' (discussed below), for many small businesses customers may contribute rather less by way of funding than do banks and other lenders; and, at the other end of the scale, it is clear that, for example, Robert Maxwell's funders were not one and the same as his customers.

Thus the argument that non-profit organisations are different from for-profits because in the former funder and consumer are separated and in the latter they are not oversimplifies reality. Non-profits may be part-funded by consumers/customers and for-profit organisations may be part-funded by people/organisations other than consumers.

Who Is the Customer?

Underlying many of the difficulties in discussion of the separation of funder and consumer/customer lies a more fundamental confusion/elasticity around the notion of the 'customer'. The fact that government funders are increasingly becoming customers buying services and also the sense in which donors to fund-raising non-profit organisations may be regarded as akin to (paying) customers have already been noted. In for-profit organisations the 'customer' is similarly difficult to define and identify. Is the customer the end-user, the immediate consumer, the person who pays or the person who makes the purchase decision?

For example, who is the customer in the case of a company manufacturing power equipment for machinery – is it the purchasing agent of the machinery manufacturer, the engineer who sets the specification or the end-user/ultimate consumer? And in some cases an industry may have no identifiable customer. As Drucker points out, in buying paper for a package, the printer, the packaging designer, the packaging converter, the customer's advertising agency, and the customer's sales and design people, all can – and do – decide what paper to buy. And yet none of them makes the buying decision itself. None of these people buys paper as such. (Drucker, 1964).

In many more, if not most, for-profit (and non-profit) industries, the funder/customer is different from the customer/consumer. For example, in Britain the major funder/customer of the pharmaceutical industry is the government funded National Health Service. Stanton's points about the effects of separation of funder and consumer in non-profit organisations might equally well be applied to consumer feedback on the value of the products supplied via the NHS by the major drug companies. Furthermore, in other industries there are many different funder customers at different levels. For example, in the clothing industry manufacturers sell to retailers who then sell to end-users; again, the consumer and the funder/customer are separated and channels for communication between the manufacturer and the consumer may be very limited.

The notion that the customer guides the business more directly in the for-profit organisation than in non-profits may oversimplify reality for other reasons. First, as noted above, a for-profit business may not only have different levels of customer but may also have many different customers at each level with different expectations and standards. What satisfies one customer may only half satisfy another. Secondly, the production process itself can affect the immediacy and thus the quality of channels of communication between customer and producer. One of the effects of the Japanese 'Just in Time' system, in which goods are produced for immediate use rather than for stock, is to bring the producer back in touch with the customer and to redefine as 'customers' those who are users but not necessarily end-users. The contrast between the Japanese JIT system and the normal production process obtaining in many companies is highlighted in the following:

> Because lot sizes are so small, and because work on one section is only carried out when it is required immediately by the next section down the line, there is rapid and direct feedback concerning quality. Moreover, the presence of 'the customer' becomes much more real. Final assembly is producing only those items which are needed by sales; it is not separated from the customer by making for finished goods stock. Similarly, each section of production becomes a surrogate customer for the section or sections which supply it, for they too are not making for intermediate stocks. (White, 1985, p.274).

Furthermore, as Moss Kanter notes, customers may not only be inside and outside the organisation but may be both customers and suppliers (Moss Kanter, 1989).

The above discussion suggests, first, that the separation of funder and customer/consumer is not peculiar to non-profit organisations but is also a characteristic displayed by some for-profits. Secondly, the definition and identification of the customer are problematic in both sectors. And finally, the relationship and channels of communication between producer and end-user are problematic independently of whether or not the consumer/customer and the funder/customer are one and the same.

In both for-profit and non-profit organisations separation of funders and end-users/consumers leads to questions about the meaning of the apparently simple term 'customer'. Some customers have rather more power than others over the purchasing/funding decision and the distinction between those who make different sorts of purchasing decisions and at what level is crucial in analysing the operation of both non-profit and for-profit organisations. Recognition of the separation of funder and consumer leads to questions concerning who is the organisation's 'guiding' customer. Does the organisation work to please, and to the agenda dictated by, the funder or the end-user? Does the organisation measure its success by the continued support of the funder or by the positive response, the continued demand, of the end-user/consumer? In the case of some non-profit and for-profit organisations the continued demand of the end-user may tell us little, except that the organisation has a local or national monopoly or that the consumer is not in a position to exercise choice or that the nature of the 'product' is such that the consumer is not in a position to judge its quality (for example, this would apply in the case of many drugs, whether supplied via the NHS or not). In these cases, the notion that consumer behaviour/demand can be used in either for-profit or non-profit organisations as an adequate guide to performance is questionable.

Rather than making over-simplified comparisons between the role of customers in different sectors, it may be more illuminating to look across sectors at organisations where different types of relationship with different customers apply. What happens in both sectors when consumers/customers and funders are separated? Does the reason for separation make any difference to management behaviour? Is it true that whenever funders and end-users are not one and the same the organisation's survival depends in large measure on the continued confidence and support of funders rather than consumers? How do different types of organisation 'build' the end-user/ consumer back into the organisation?

5
The Effects of Charitable Status

'Managing without profit' is sometimes run together in the literature with charitable status. However, although all non-profit organisations, in some sense, 'manage without profit', not all non-profit organisations are registered charities. This chapter considers some organisational and management characteristics of non-profits which stem primarily from charitable status and which therefore apply to some but not all such organisations.

Managing Boards

Professionals and volunteers. One feature characteristic of many, but not all, non-profit organisations which stems primarily from charitable status, is the separation between volunteer, unremunerated trustees legally responsible for the organisation and staff paid to manage the organisation.

Various writers suggest that the organisational structure of charities, which requires volunteer trustees/a Board directing professional managers who are paid to manage but have no legal power to determine policy, creates an inherent problem in the management of such organisations. In many ways, however, the problems created by this structure are no different from those of the for-profit organisation with a non-executive Board of directors.

Drucker's description of the Board in for-profit organisations could well be a description of that in a charity:

> *In reality the Board as conceived by the law-maker is at best a tired fiction. It is perhaps not too much to say that it has become a shadow king. In most of the large companies it has in effect been deposed and its place taken by executive management... Or the Board may have become a mere showcase, a place to inject distinguished names, without information, influence or desire for power.*
> (Drucker, 1968, p.217).

The problematic role of such a Board has been much discussed and is usually attributed to the divorce of ownership and control which has occurred in this century. In non-profit organisations the same difficulties are apparent but they cannot be attributed to the separation of financial ownership from control. Given the similar problems in both types of organisation, it may be suggested that problems in the role of the Board stem not so much from the divorce of ownership and control or from charitable status per se but rather from the growth and claims of professional management.

Various studies have shown that in reality in non-profit organisations the Chief Executive 'educates' or leads the Board. In such organisations there is an informal structure of control which mirrors (ie reverses) the formal structure but which is rarely openly acknowledged (Harris, 1992; Stanton, 1970; Senor, 1965; Kramer, 1965; Middleton, 1987).

Multiple interests. Non-profit Boards are sometimes presented as being more complicated than those of for-profit organisations insofar as non-profit organisations have multiple constituencies represented on their Boards. Non-profit Board members are often selected to 'represent' or to cement relationships with the multiple constituencies and stakeholders of the organisation – government funders, donors, consumers, other related voluntary organisations. Board members may also be selected to provide the organisation with credibility and legitimacy, eg for fund-raising purposes.

The result of these criteria for selection may be not only that Board members are already busy people but also that they have a limited understanding of the work of the organisation, of the professional values of the staff and of the realities of managing a non-profit organisation. Furthermore, their primary allegiance may be to their own organisation and they may regard sitting on the non-profit Board as a way of protecting or representing their own organisation's interests (Leat *et al.*, 1981; Harris, 1992).

But whether these characteristics of some non-profit Boards are any different from those of for-profit Boards is debatable. Boards of large, modern for-profit corporations are likely to contain diverse and sometimes overlapping interests and allegiances. The notion that such a Board 'represents the shareholders' is as much an over- simplification as is the notion that the non-profit Board represents the membership. In larger modern for-profit organisations not only are ownership and control divorced but also ownership is dispersed, with minority and majority, individual and institutional, shareholders engaged in often complex and shifting coalitions and alliances (Scott, 1985). By comparison, the various allegiances of non-profit Board members may appear less problematic.

Payment and non-payment. A more significant difference between the non-profit and for-profit Boards may be that members of the former are unpaid whereas members of the latter are likely to be well-rewarded for their involvement. The fact that non-profit Board members are, by law, unpaid volunteers may have a variety of consequences which affect the management of nonprofit organisations and, in particular, the relationships and roles of Board members and staff. First, as unpaid volunteers, Board members may have limited time for meetings and for preparation. This may hinder their scope for real involvement in complex decisions and require considerable delegation to staff in the intervals between relatively infrequent meetings. Secondly, as volunteers themselves and as trustees of a charity/non-profit organisation, Board members may explicitly or implicitly believe that staff pay and hours should also include a voluntary element and may be resistant to the notion of offering competitive salaries. Thirdly, in some charities/non-profits the ethos of voluntarism, subscribed to and exemplified by Board members, may lead them to distance themselves from the responsibilities of being employers leaving the employment function to staff themselves to handle (Harris, 1992). More generally, the volunteer trustees of some charities/non-profits may display a bias against 'managerialism' and/or the need for professional staff.

Social distance. One further difficulty in charities/non-profit organisations may stem from the fact that Board members tend to be drawn from limited social strata which are very different from those of both staff and users of the organisation's services (Kramer, 1965). That charity trustees must be volunteers may contribute to this preponderance of trustees from higher social strata insofar as only those who have some other source of income or a job or position which permits paid time off are likely to be available. Some charities have recently begun to include as expenses a sum for 'lost earnings'. This may enlarge the potential social pool from which trustees are drawn, but is probably on the margins of legality within British charity law.

Management implications. What effects do these characteristics of Boards of charity/non-profit organisations have on the management of such organisations?

Drucker, discussing the functions of the Board in for-profit organisations, suggests that there are some functions which only a Board can discharge. These include approving the organisation's mission, its objectives and the measurements it develops to judge its progress towards these objectives. The role of the Board is also to look critically at the organisation's financial planning and to act as the 'Supreme Court' in relation to organisational problems. Finally, it is the role of the Board to 'watch the spirit of the organisation' – to make sure that it develops managers and that its rewards to management strengthen the organisation and direct it towards its objectives (Drucker, 1968).

On this analysis the weakness of the volunteer/charity Board may be precisely that it is composed of volunteers with limited time and, in some cases, a commitment to voluntarism and/or a bias against professional management. Its strength, on the other hand, may be that its members are often, for the reasons noted above, 'distanced' from the organisation.

> *The Board must be ... detached from operations ... the Board will be stronger and more effective if it is genuinely an 'outside' Board.'... it is to the advantage of the Board in the large business that its members do not know the details.* (ibid, p.218).

However, Drucker goes on to emphasise two further important points which may, in practice, undermine this apparent strength. First, he argues that Board members must be carefully selected. The organisation needs '... Board members whose experience, outlook and interests are different from those of management. This cannot be obtained by getting representatives of the company's bankers, suppliers and customers'. Secondly, 'to get the kind of people the company needs, Board membership will have to be made financially attractive'.

Creating an effective Board is, according to Drucker, one of the most important things the paid management staff can do. To what extent this can be achieved in charities and non-profit organisations is debatable. One of Drucker's major conditions (payment) is legally incompatible with charitable status, and another is only partially fulfilled insofar as Board members tend to be socially different from management but, at the same time, tend, increasingly, to be representatives of funders, 'competitors' and consumers.

It is worth noting here that when the British Government decided to set up NHS trusts – which could on other criteria have been regarded as charities – it considered it necessary to pay trustees, thus effectively ruling out the possibility, and the advantages, of charitable status. And many charities increasingly 'stretch' the law by compensating trustees for loss of earnings in order to secure the participation of people who could not otherwise afford to be involved.

Despite these apparent disadvantages of the charity Board, in his later work Drucker has argued that in strategic planning and effectiveness of the Board, non-profit organisations are '... practising what most American businesses only preach' (Drucker, 1990). Whatever the situation in the United States, various British research studies suggest that the strong 'challenging' Board is far from common. The more usual pattern is a Board in awe of staff or avoiding conflict (which in itself may be part of the organisational culture of non-profit organisations) by an implicit understanding that it should not 'interfere' in the management of the organisation (Harris, 1992).

Non-profit and For-profit Boards – Similarities

When looked at more closely, it appears that modern for-profit Boards and non-profit charity Boards have in practice rather more in common than might be assumed. The combination of diverse interests typical of the non-profit Board may be similar to the growing significance of for-profit companies with no dominant ownership. Even if ownership is dominated by a small number of well-informed and powerful financial intermediaries:

> *This group of, say, 20 large shareholders will collectively hold a majority or substantial minority of shares, but are too diverse to vote this in a co-ordinated way... The board will reflect the constellation of interests and is unable to achieve the autonomy from particular stockholder interests which is characterisitic of management control, yet the dominant shareholders do not constitute a cohesive controlling group'* (Scott, 1985, p.141-2).

And in both the non-profit and the for-profit organisation managers may gain autonomy/control both from the diversity of board interests and from their own control of information.

The following description of the Board of a modern for-profit organisation with diverse interests represented on its Board might apply equally to the workings of a non-profit Board:

> In the 'struggle for control' executives are able to structure the information received by board directors. They may, for example, seek generalised approval for a course of action by presenting the minimum of detail and limiting the options available to their fellow directors. Shareholder and financial representatives on the board may in fact be prepared to encourage such manoeuvring as a way of controlling executives who have to work hard and efficiently to pre-empt board decisions... so long as a company successfully meets its financial targets they will have no incentive to disrupt executive strategies (ibid, p.143).

Centrality of Substantive Intangible Mission

Other supposedly distinctive characteristics of charities which flow from charitable status are, first, that charities' missions are central to their legal status and raison d'etre and, secondly, that their missions are likely to be intangible. For-profit organisations, by contrast, are alleged to have only one goal – profit maximisation.

The fact that a substantive mission – relieving poverty, services to deaf people, educating young people – is central to charitable status and the very raison d'etre of a charitable organisation is alleged to have several consequences for management. For example, Drucker argues that non-profit organisations are better managed than for-profits insofar as the centrality of their mission means that they are more likely to start from a well-defined purpose and work on from there. By contrast, he suggests, for-profits start from a budget rather than a mission (Drucker, 1990).

But whatever the theory and whatever the situation in the United States, the general impression in Britain is that charities muddle on with something very far from a clearly defined mission. Indeed for good legal reasons a broad vague mission is likely to be deliberately built into the organisation's deeds at the time of charitable registration.

A second consequence of the charity's centrality of mission is that it supposedly has less flexibility in resource allocation and 'direction' than a for-profit organisation which can change its direction and its methods/routes so long as it continues to deliver profit (Moss Kanter and Summers, 1987). In reality, as noted above, many charity 'mission' statements are deliberately broad enough to leave the organisation with a great deal of flexibility and, in any case, charities have shown themselves to be adept at changing their mission to ensure survival. The Young Men's Christian Association, for example, has managed to transform itself into an organisation serving non-Christian men and women!

Young argues that one of the positive features of the centrality of mission in charities/non-profits is that such organisations stay with their mission and do not diversify into businesses they know nothing about (Young, 1985). Again, this may be true in the United States but in Britain some charities in recent years have only too readily diversified into other fields – unemployment being the major example – in an effort to secure funding, whatever the cost in relation to both pursuit of their central mission and longer-term organisational survival.

More fundamentally, it may be argued that it is the intangibility of the mission of a non-profit organisation which creates greater difficulties in management as compared with those in for-profits whose goal, it is alleged, is tangible, ie profit maximisation. Certainly, as noted above, the mission of most if not all charities is intangible, but many for-profits have intangible goals such as 'serving the customer' or 'producing quality goods at prices the customer can afford' – even if *one* measure of success is then sales and profit. For some for-profits at some stages, short-term profit may be less significant than other less tangible goals.

Again, just as for-profit companies may be moving closer to non-profits in that they are increasingly putting intangible goals such as quality or service before short-term profit maximisation, so non-profits may increasingly move closer to for-profits in putting financial viability higher up their agendas. In the new contract culture, non-profit organisations may have to learn to juggle the intangible goals of public benefit/service with the more tangible objectives of acquiring contracts and satisfying a variety of paying and non-paying customers within the constraints of the real cost of financial survival. If, as Drucker argues, profit is nothing more than the real cost of staying in business, then profit is likely to be of increasing concern to non-profit and for-profit organisations alike.

This brief review of organisational characteristics stemming from charitable status suggests that these characteristics are complex and variable in effect. Furthermore, the above discussion indicates that, on closer consideration, organisational characteristics supposedly stemming from charitable status are not peculiar to charity non-profit organisations but are also displayed by other organisations both non-profit and for-profit.

6
Professionals, Paid Staff and Volunteers.

As noted above, charitable status necessarily implies a public benefit mission. Another characteristic of non-profit organisations which is related to, but distinguishable from, their intangible public benefit mission is the role of professionals within the organisation.

The preponderance of professionals or 'knowledge workers', claiming specialist expertise which may not be possessed by senior managers or Board, is sometimes assumed to create distinctive management problems in non-profit organisations. In addition, these organisations may involve volunteers whose management may present special problems. In the United States the non-profit sector is the largest employer/manager involving more than 80 million people as staff and volunteers. Volunteer time alone is equivalent to 10 million full-time jobs (Drucker, 1989). In Britain 23 million people volunteer each year, with 10 million people giving an estimated 100 million volunteer hours each week (Volunteer Centre, 1991).

But these aggregate figures can give a misleading impression. In Britain the majority of non-profit organisations employ no paid staff and involve few volunteers while a small proportion of the largest non-profits employ large numbers of paid staff and involve large numbers of volunteers.

A recent survey of 185 top charities suggested that they had 392,006 people working for them, an average of over 2,000 per organisation. Only two of these 185 top charities employed no paid staff and relied entirely on volunteers. The other 183 charities employed 36,911 people, an average of 202 per organisation. But these paid staff were not evenly spread throughout the organisations surveyed. Child welfare organisations had the highest average number of paid staff, with 840 per organisation; arts organisations had the second highest average of 665. In addition to staff employed and paid by the organisation itself, 37 charities had help from a total of 727 staff seconded from other organisations. The majority of organisations also involved volunteers; 122 had had 352,403 volunteers working for them at some time during the previous year, an average of 2,889 per charity. Again, these volunteers were not evenly spread throughout the different areas of work; the 3 environmental and heritage organisations responding to the survey involved an average of 11,534 voluteers each! (Day 1991). Thus, even among charities, there is considerable variation in the numbers and proportions of paid staff and volunteers involved.

There are three distinct but related aspects to the management of staff in non-profit organisations: managing professionals and knowledge workers, managing unpaid part-time volunteers and managing the interaction of both paid and unpaid workers, volunteers and professionals, in the same organisation. If an organisation employs no paid staff it does not have to address the last problem but may nevertheless have to grapple with the first insofar as many volunteers are knowledge workers in their paid employment and may bring the attitudes and expectations of knowledge workers to their work as volunteers.

Managing Professionals and Knowledge Workers.

Standards and autonomy. One problem which may be exacerbated by a high proportion of professional staff is that of measuring outcomes. This is likely to be especially true in social work organisations where outcomes are notoriously difficult to measure, but it may occur in any non-profit organisation if the (specialist/professional) knowledge to devise outcome measures is not available to funders, customers/users and indeed to sections of management. Professional 'producers' are likely to be more knowledgeable than those they supposedly serve and may therefore be judge and jury over their own products and services.

Secondly, and closely related, professionals bring with them professional values. These include a strong emphasis on autonomy to make their own judgements and manage their own work in accordance with professional values and with minimum interference from others.

In reality, of course, these problems are not peculiar to nonprofit organisations. Many parts of the for-profit sector are increasingly dominated by professionals and 'knowledge workers' and, to that extent, the management difficultes created by a preponderance of professionals are experienced by organisations in both sectors. For example, one of the several characteristics which made Apple, especially in its early years, more like a voluntary organisation than a stereotypical for-profit organisation was that it was dominated by young, highly individual professional computer 'wizards' dedicated to changing the world through the application of their specialist skills (Scully, 1989).

The implications for management in non-profit and, increasingly, in for-profit organisations are considerable. Noting that the voluntary sector is a 'magnet' for professionals, educators and researchers, Young suggests: 'Management control over a workforce of professionals is thus successfully exerted not so much by coercion or even by material reward as by establishing a supportive environment, respecting domains of professional autonomy, and achieving professional consensus in important decisions' (Young, 1985, quoted in Mason, 1990, p.372). And Drucker (1990) states that:

> Managing the knowledge worker for productivity is the challenge ahead for American management. The non-profits are showing us how to do that. It requires a clear mission, careful placement and continuous learning and teaching, management by objectives and self-control, in demands but corresponding responsibility and accountability for performance and results.

The above are problems which many for-profit organisations share with non-profits. But professionals and other staff have first to be recruited and, second, to be retained by, among other things, material inducements – and it is in this area that non-profit organisations may face particular problems.

Recruiting and Retaining Professionals and Other Paid Staff.

Data on paid staff employed by non-profit organisations in Britain are patchy and unsystematic, but efforts are currently being made to remedy this. One of the many difficulties in obtaining such data is that, because these organisations are undergoing rapid change, not least as a result of contracting, data are likely to be out-of-date as soon as they are published. The following data are drawn from a survey conducted in 1989 by the Manufacturing Science and Finance Union. Things have no doubt changed since then, but the figures may nevertheless give a broad indication of the position of nonprofit organisations relative to other sectors. All of the data below should be read in the light of the fact that an estimated 71% of voluntary organisation employees are women.

Pay and benefits. Although pay may not be the only factor which recruits and retains staff the total employment package offered by an organisation will certainly be important.

25% of staff covered by the MSF survey earned less than £9,000 per annum, 50% between £9,000 and £13,000 and the remaining 25% over £13,000. By contrast, the figures for all non-manual employees (ie in all sectors) suggest that almost half (44%) earn over £13,000, just over a quarter (27%) earn between £9,000 and £13,000, and between one quarter and one-third (29%) earn under

£9,000 (Ball, 1992).

Thus it appears that pay in the non-profit sector is lower than in other sectors, which may simply reflect the fact that non-profit organisations tend to be small and thus senior jobs carry less responsibility. Pay structures in the non-profit sector are also flatter, which may reflect a less hierarchical structure in some organisations and/or a deliberate policy of narrower pay differentials.

It is worth noting that although senior staff in non-profit organisations may be worse off than their counterparts in other sectors, this does not apply to many junior managers who, outside London, are on average 2% better paid than those in the private for-profit sector. Clerical workers in non-profit organisations tend to be paid close to the market rate (Ball, 1992).

Many non-profit sector staff not only receive lower pay than they might expect elsewhere but they are also unlikely to receive other benefits to compensate for this. One of the few benefits which is more likely to be available in voluntary as opposed to private sector organisations is paternity leave but this is rare in both sectors (Ball, 1992).

Job security is another significant and particularly difficult area for organisations dependent upon funding from sources over which they have little direct control.

Finding the right mix of pay and other benefits (and differentials) at a price which is affordable is important to all organisations in whatever sector. The right package may well be different for different workers and, in addition, may change over time. In future many professionals and knowledge workers, previously relatively immune from fears of unemployment, may place greater emphasis on job security and redundancy packages than on annual salary. But in offering both pay and benefit packages non-profit organisations may operate at a disadvantage as compared with many for-profit organisations.

First, many non-profits are not free to determine their own pay levels or even to follow the market. Apart from the obvious point that, like for-profit organisations, non-profits are constrained by the budget of what is affordable, they may be additionally constrained in determining pay levels insofar as the level or the scale is set by the funder; some non-profits in receipt of local authority funding are required to operate policies analogous to local authority pay regimes (Ball, 1992).

Another reason why non-profit organisations may be constrained in what they can pay their staff stems from public (and sometimes board) expectations of the level of pay which is 'appropriate' for the staff of charities. Public acceptability of top people's pay has recently become an increasingly important issue for some for-profit organisations and was considered by the Cadbury Committee on corporate governance. But in general the public, even if they are shareholders, can impose few, if any, sanctions on for-profit organisations. For non-profits dependent upon fund-raising from the general public or on grants from publicly elected and accountable government bodies, the sanctions supported by those who disapprove of 'high' pay may be much more easily applied. Recently, in the United States the Director of United Way, a major fund-raising charity, was forced to resign after his allegedly over-generous salary and other benefits were revealed. The issue was widely reported and discussed in the media, and there were fears that one result could be loss of public confidence in the whole organisation and its fund-raising activities.

Secondly, non-profit organisations may face particular difficulties in offering employees and potential employees other benefits to compensate for possibly lower levels of pay. Like other small organisations in whatever sector, some nonprofits may have difficulty in meeting the costs of employment benefits such as maternity leave and pensions. But, in addition, non-profits are often constrained both by what the funder will accept as a reasonable overhead and by the chronic insecurity of their funding, whether from government, charitable trusts or from the general public.

Thirdly, and closely related, non-profit organisations may face particular difficulties in providing job security and adequate redundancy arrangements. Given the short-term and unstable nature of voluntary sector funding, providing job security is especially difficult. In addition, some voluntary organisations see their role as starting new projects and then 'floating' them off to independence with not always beneficial effects for their employees:

> In the private sector it is clear that such arrangements would be unlawful, either because the legal entity of a company remains the same when it is transferred by an acquisition of shares or because the Transfer of Undertakings (Protection of Employment) Regulations 1991 would apply.'
> (Ball, 1992, p.79).

However, it is likely that the current lack of clarity in the application of employment legislation to non-profit organisations will be removed under European law. Employees may benefit from such clarification, but the problem for non-profits will then become one of finding funding to implement these laws.

Finally, many non-profit organisations may face particular difficulties in providing adequate employment packages because of organisational values which put equality above differentials. This may be one reason for the flatter pay structures displayed by many of them. But, although the values of many non-profit organisations may emphasise absence of differentials, the realities of the labour market may require differentials if staff are to be recruited. In a period of recession this conflict may not be apparent, but when competition for senior staff increases non-profits may have to make uncomfortable choices which raise issues at the very heart of the organisation.

The conclusion to be drawn is that a preponderance of professionals and knowledge workers cannot be regarded as a distinctive characteristic of non-profit organisations. But although non-profits share with many for-profit organisations the special problems involved in managing professionals and knowledge workers, they may face some additional and possibly distinctive problems in this area.

Volunteers: A Distinctive Ingredient, Special Problems?

To the lay person voluntary or non-profit organisations are more or less synonymous with organisations composed of volunteers. And at first glance the presence of volunteers does indeed seem to constitute a distinctive characteristic of non-profit organisations and one which is likely to present special management problems.

As noted above, in reality, some non-profit organisations are totally dependent upon volunteer labour, others are composed solely of (volunteer) members, and others involve no volunteers. Even so, it may be argued, the contribution of volunteers is an option for all non-profit organisations, whereas it is highly unlikely (though presumably not theoretically impossible) that a for-profit organisation could sustain volunteer involvement.

Paying some attention to the management of volunteers is important for several reasons. As noted at the beginning of this chapter, volunteers play an important role as a source of labour in some but not all non-profit organisations. Volunteers are also one source of the supposed cost advantage of some non-profits – an advantage which often disappears when the costs of managing volunteers are taken into account. Volunteers are also important insofar as their involvement is part of the ideology of some non-profits – a feature which is not found in any for-profits and one which may impose particular management problems peculiar to non-profits. Furthermore, the presence of volunteers and their management are not only interesting in themselves but may also have effects on the organisation and on the management of paid workers.

Perhaps most significantly, however, understanding volunteer motivation and involvement may shed new light on motivating and managing all workers in all modern organisations in which material rewards and sanctions are increasingly seen as inadequate management tools. In the past volunteers were largely seen as altruistic, coming in and remaining because of what they brought to the organisation in the form of a desire to do good. Now, however, non-profit organisations are increasingly adopting a transactional approach in which the organisation feels obliged to give volunteers something in return:

> *Non-profits used to say 'we don't pay volunteers so we cannot make demands upon them.' Now they are more likely to say 'Volunteers must get far greater satisfaction from their accomplishments and make a greater contribution precisely because they do not get a pay cheque"* (Drucker, 1989, p.90).

Elsewhere Drucker argues that for-profit managers will not in future be able to rely on material rewards nor on old notions of management and authority in motivating and managing staff.

What is needed, he argues, is a new style of management in which material rewards are less significant and the idea of the boss issuing orders and sanctions is not appropriate. It is worth noting here that this 'new' style of management may accord rather more closely with what managers themselves actually look for in work. In a study of British managers, Hansen found that earning a substantial amount of money ranked well below the freedom to carry out their own ideas, a chance for originality and initiative, and work with associates they personally liked (Hansen, 1976). With lower pay levels for many paid staff and with no money to motivate and no fear of loss of income to sanction volunteers, non-profit organisations may have experience of considerable value in understanding new styles of management.

But the presence of volunteers creates its own management difficulties. As Willis points out, volunteers do not magically appear; they must be planned for, their involvement must have an organisational logic, there must be a clear philosophy of why they are to be involved and what they are there to do and how their tasks and responsibilities relate to those of paid staff. Without this type of strategic planning, the presence of volunteers is likely to create more problems than it solves. The tasks of recruiting, selecting, matching, supporting, coordinating and evaluating volunteers must also be planned for and appropriate resources allocated to these tasks (Willis, 1992). Volunteers may be unpaid but they are not cost-free in management terms. In addition, apart from the direct costs of paying expenses and ensuring their health and safety and the health and safety of those they work with, volunteers may present thorny legal liability, contractual and tax problems. On top of these costs the presence of volunteers may create other less obvious management problems.

The likelihood of being a volunteer increases with income and educational qualifications, and this in itself may have important organisational and management implications insofar as such people are not only capable of, and used to, taking responsibility for skilled work but are also the social equals rather than socially subordinate to paid managers. Interestingly, people in paid work are more likely to volunteer than those without work.

On average the 'typical' volunteer spends only 2.7 hours a week on volunteer activity (Volunteer Centre, 1991). While this average undoubtedly conceals wide variations among types of organisation, areas of activity and among volunteers, it does suggest that what managers are dealing with are large numbers of people giving relatively small amounts of time. This fact alone is likely to impose significant demands on managers.

If volunteering is seen as transactional rather than altruistic – as much a matter of what the volunteer gets from the organisation as what he/she gives – then rewards must also be provided. This is, of course, true in managing all workers in all organisations but it is especially true of volunteers precisely because their rewards cannot simply be dealt with by offering more money. Arguably, for-profit organisations have placed too much emphasis on pay and neglected the development of other rewards for workers. The new management texts emphasise the need to provide workers with opportunities for responsibility, self-development, learning, creativity and so on. In developing these 'new' rewards, for-profit organisations may find it useful to look more closely at non-profit organisations where structures providing such rewards may already be in place, sometimes bringing with them other management problems. What, then, are the satisfactions and dissatisfactions of working without pay?

The volunteers studied by Sills found satisfaction in the opportunities for self-fulfilment which they felt volunteer work gave them. 'Opportunity for self-fulfilment' took various forms. For some the opportunity to do good, to do something worthwhile, was important, for others contact with professionals, being treated as an equal, or acquiring skills and being good at using them were what mattered. Sills also identified participation in a social movement – a feeling of belonging, of working together with others, of participation in achieving change for the better – as a key satisfaction of being a volunteer (Sills, 1957).

The volunteers responding to the Volunteer Centre UK survey mentioned satisfactions such as seeing results (possibly related to the high proportion involved in fund-raising – one of the few tangible outcomes in volunteer work?). Half of all volunteers said that they gained satisfaction from the social aspects of their work – meeting people and making new friends. A sense of personal achievement was also important to these volunteers. Older volunteers in particular valued the opportunity to do something they were good at and younger ones gained satisfaction from learning new skills and/or obtaining a recognised qualification.

But there were also drawbacks for some volunteers. Over 65% felt that their volunteering could be better organised and a sizeable minority of volunteers identified a mismatch between the tasks they were asked to do and those that they were willing to do. Thirty per cent said they could not always cope with the things they were asked to do, and a further 20% said they did not do the things they wanted to (Volunteer Centre UK 1991). In addition, around one quarter felt that their efforts were not always appreciated.

Both the satisfactions and the costs of volunteering bear a striking similarity to Drucker's three conditions for work in the future: jobs must make achievement possible and must provide for feedback and for continuous learning. But the data above also suggest that volunteer managers must be careful to fit the right person to the right job suited to his/her abilities. This may create management difficulties if time has to be spent finding jobs for people rather than people for jobs. Which comes first: volunteer satisfaction or the efficient and effective performance of organisational tasks?

As Young points out, the presence of volunteers may create, or exacerbate, problems for non-profit organisations in relating rewards to performance. By definition volunteers are not sensitive to financial inducements and in addition may demand considerable discretion in what they do freely and without reward. Unless two different approaches are to be taken to the performance of volunteers and that of paid staff the 'freedom' of volunteers is likely to have important implications for the assessment and management of the work of the whole organisation (Young, 1987).

Secondly, the presence of volunteers, some of whom may be involved primarily for the rewards of sociability, may create a 'clubby' work environment. This sociable ethos may serve an important function in sustaining volunteers, but may lead to loss of coherence and service oriented behaviour in the organisation as a whole. If the organisational ethos also requires the involvement of volunteers not for what they can contribute to the achievement of the organisation's goals but rather for social or humanitarian reasons or as therapy for the volunteers themselves, further difficulties may arise. In such situations the very notion of performance evaluation and standards may come to be seen as inappropriate. These are difficult issues for many non-profit organisations and relate to pursuit of their social mission both inside and outside the organisation. If the organisation's mission is to help deaf or mentally ill people, then should it not pursue this mission in its employment and volunteer involvement practices? Should it not first 'practice what it preaches'?

In addition, the satisfaction of working without pay appears to depend upon an egalitarian participative organisational framework – an ethos which many writers have identified as being particularly prevalent in non-profit organisations. But the presence of volunteers and their need for participation and equality, combined with paid professional staff and their need for autonomy, as well as the 'ambiguous' relationship between staff and Board, may produce a potent mix from which organisational chaos may all too easily emerge.

7
Organisational Ethos: Egalitarianism and Participation

A number of writers have noted an ethos of egalitarianism and participation as one characteristic of non-profit organisations which is likely to present particular management constraints and problems.

The existence of this type of egalitarian ethos in bureaucratic, and often hierarchical non-profit organisations may be related to Billis's characterisation of voluntary organisations as occupying an ambiguous zone between that of associations which are affective, expressive and democratic and bureaucracies which are instrumental and managed. The position of voluntary organisations in this ambiguous zone, Billis argues, sheds light on the practical management problems in such organisations 'which can be seen as resulting from the tensions of adhering both to the rules of the game of the associational world (democratic elections, voting, etc) and those of the bureaucratic world (managerial command structures, contracts of employment, etc)' (Billis, 1990).

Equal Opportunities

At one level all organisations, for-profit and non-profit, must be egalitarian in the sense that they must comply with equal opportunities legislation. Indeed all organisations may have much to learn from each other about problems and successes in implementing such legislation. However, non-profits may face particular pressures and problems in implementing equal opportunity policies.

First, non-profits may experience greater pressure to be 'more equal' and to achieve this equality faster precisely because of their public benefit mission and their emphasis on overcoming social disadvantage. For-profit organisations, on the other hand, do not pretend to be about reducing social disadvantage and to that extent may gain extra marks for promoting equal opportunities whereas non-profit organisations may only lose marks for failing to do so. A second source of pressure for some non-profit organisations stems from the fact that equal opportunities may be as much a matter of process as of results. For these organisations women or ethnic minority workers must not simply be employed but must be developed and empowered as part of the organisation's mission.

On top of these additional pressures to be more equal than others, non-profit organisations may experience particular difficulties in meeting the cost of implementing equal opportunities policies. These costs, not necessarily covered by funders, include both tangible costs (the cost of adapting a building for disabled workers for example) and intangible costs (the extra time which may be involved in following strict equal opportunities procedures in recruiting staff).

In addition, some non-profits may also be required or concerned to implement equal access for users as well as equal opportunities policies for staff and volunteers (see below for further discussion of this point).

Beyond Equal Opportunities

Many non-profit organisations go beyond merely complying with equal opportunities legislation and display a more general organisational ethos of egalitarianism and participation. This wider emphasis may be seen as a product of their public benefit mission and the preponderance of professionals and knowledge workers as well as the presence of volunteers. For different reasons both volunteers and professionals may expect or demand the right to control not merely over their own work but also over the values, objectives and direction of the organisation.

An ethos of shared power between all parties within the organisation – volunteer Board members, paid staff and volunteer workers – has obvious implications for the autonomy and tasks of senior management. In some organisations these tasks may be further complicated by the existence of local branches/federations. The egalitarian ethos requires that local organisations are seen to be autonomous but in reality, in order to ensure maintenance of standards and consistency, there is likely to be some central direction – whether acknowledged or not. The tension between the central/national organisation and the local 'branches' may be further heightened if the former tends towards the bureaucratic hierarchical end of the spectrum and the latter are closer to the associational end. The result is likely to be different expectations, standards and tolerance of participation and egalitarianism.

Egalitarianism and Participation: A Distinctive Characteristic?

A wider egalitarian/participative ethos is not characteristic of all non-profit organisations; nor is it peculiar to such organisations. For-profit organisations may in different degrees and forms display such an ethos, especially, but not solely, where there is a large proportion of professional/specialist staff. Indeed, some of the 'new' management texts have argued that the only way to manage well, to manage for success, in future is to remove barriers and positively promote more egalitarian and participative practices (Peters and Austin, 1985; Moss Kanter, 1989).

In the past egalitarian/ participative approaches to management – worker control – were largely based on arguments about the benefits of improving the quality of working life. More recently, however, new computerised process technologies have encouraged reconsideration of work flows and roles. Achieving greater 'worker control' is no longer a matter of improving the quality of life – an optional 'add-on' – but is rather one of matching management practice to process in order to ensure maximum efficiency and minimum waste. Walton and Susman in a *Harvard Business Review* article entitled 'People policies for the new machines' argue that advanced manufacturing technology may lead to increases in: interdependencies between functions, skill requirements, the speed, scope and costs of error, the sensitivity of performance to variation in skill, knowledge and attitudes, the pace of dynamic change and development, capital investment per employee and dependence upon smaller numbers of skilled people. In these circumstances, they argue, management practices must include greater emphasis on multi-skilling, teamwork and greater worker autonomy within a flexible, highly skilled and committed workforce (Walton and Susman, 1987).

Again, then, it may be that the management strategies and dilemmas of for-profit organisations will increasingly become more like those of non-profit organisations heavily dominated by professionals and volunteers who, for different reasons, also expect a high degree of autonomy and participation. Managing by commitment to core organisational tasks, values and quality standards may become a key priority for organisations in both sectors.

Managing Conflict

Emphasis on the egalitarian/participative ethos to which many non-profit organisations subscribe, at least in theory, raises the issue of how these organisations manage to survive with so many different individual interests potentially pulling in different directions? Or to put it somewhat differently: how is conflict managed in non-profit organisations and who/what determines the things that happen in such organisations? This question is not only about the respective roles and power of staff and volunteers but also about the role of those supposedly in control – the Board.

The answer to these questions is definitely not that conflict does not exist within non-profit organisations. Many non-profits may be charities but in their everyday internal activities and relationships they do not necessarily display unremitting consensus, tolerance and generosity. Despite their supposed adherence to a common cause and to participation and egalitarianism, conflict may arise between staff and Board, within the Board, between different groups of staff, between staff and volunteers, between volunteers and between Board and volunteers. Indeed, it might be argued that it is precisely because each group is convinced that it has right on its side as well as the right to influence the direction of the organisation that conflict is likely to occur and, when it does, to be especially bitter.

The answer to the question of what keeps such organisations together is probably much the same as it is in for-profit organisations where conflicts arise within the Board, between Board and staff, and between different groups of staff. The simplest answer is that each party has a stake in the survival and smooth functioning of the organisation; no one has much to gain if the organisation collapses.

Beyond that simple answer, however, is the fact that top management has considerable influence in diverting conflict. Management creates the rules, the systems and procedures which in themselves ensure a general conformity. Management constructs recruitment criteria and procedures which may do a considerable amount to avoid potential conflict; people are selected because they are likely to 'fit into the team', 'to make a positive contribution' to the organisation. Volunteers too are increasingly subject to selection procedures which may be presented as being for the volunteer's benefit but are equally concerned with ensuring that the organisation gets only those people with whom it can 'cope'. Promotion and reward systems, whether monetary or not, further reinforce certain values and ways of doing things. Similarly, training informs people as to what is expected of them and inculcates the right methods and approaches; again, there is increasing emphasis on the need for more training of volunteers.

And, as in for-profit organisations, in non-profit organisations:

> Many of the most dramatic political battles take place as senior executives fight for promotion or empires, or try to change the direction which the organisation is taking' (Lee, 1985).

Interestingly too, as in for-profits, the Board may be among the last to know when something is going seriously wrong in the non-profit organisation.

8
Constituencies and Accountability

One of the alleged differences between for-profit organisations and public service non-profit organisations, dependent upon donors and funders, is that the latter have to satisfy a wider variety of constituencies and/or are expected to be more accountable than the former. For example, Drucker argues that, because the public service institution has no results out of which it is paid, it follows that

> ... *any constituent, no matter how marginal, has in effect a veto power. A public service institution has to satisfy everyone; certainly it cannot afford to alienate anyone* (Drucker, 1985).

According to Drucker, this need to respond to multiple constituencies is a distinctive feature of public service organisations. In for-profit organisations, he argues, one constituency – the customer – overrides all others; if the organisation satisfies the customer all other constituents will be satisfied. If Drucker's analysis were correct this would certainly constitute a fundamental difference between management of non-profit and for-profit organisations and would make management of the former an up-hill battle!

But Drucker's analysis is arguably an over-simplification of the nature of many modern for-profit organisations and of the social and political environment in which they operate. For one thing, modern corporate theory recognises that the firm is a coalition of participants with disparate demands. The constituencies of for-profit organisations may include customers, banks and other lenders, shareholders, employees, trade unions, central and local government planning and regulatory bodies (and in some cases funders/subsidisers), consumer and environmental lobby groups, suppliers, distributors as well as other related industries/firms (for example, manufacturers of computer hardware dependent upon the confidence and co-operation of computer software firms to make their product saleable).

A second objection to Drucker's notion of the customer as king is that it oversimplifies the realities of markets. Perfect competition in which the customer is a powerful price fixer rarely exists outside textbooks. Much more common today are monopolies and oligopolies. In these types of market and with growing expenditure by producers on advertising the producer rather than the customer is sovereign.

Drucker's argument that the different agendas of each of these groups can be reconciled under the banner of keeping the customer happy may amount to nothing more than the truism that when everyone's interests are balanced everyone is happy. This conceals the difficult decisions and compromises involved in achieving that balance. For example, shareholders may be more interested in short- or long-term return on capital invested; managers may be more interested in maximising sales or growth; customers may be interested in low prices, whereas suppliers may be interested in obtaining the highest possible price for their goods. Government and consumer and environmental lobby groups may be less interested in prices and profits and more interested in wider social and economic costs and benefits.

Before looking more closely at the different constituencies to which non-profit organisations are accountable it is worth making two general points.

First, as Young and Finch point out the reality is that non-profit organisations have varying degrees of 'organisational slack'. In other words, some are better positioned than others in terms of resources, reserves and external obligations 'to indulge their own internally conceived goal structures' (Young and Finch, 1977). Different degrees of organisational slack give organisations different key constituencies and different degrees of freedom to 'ignore' what would be constraining constituencies for another organisation.

Organisations not only have different key constituencies but these constituencies may exercise different degrees of constraint on the organisation's goals and practices. Some constituencies may be paid lip service, others may be taken very seriously. The power of constituents to influence the non-profit organisation cannot be related solely to financial power/significance to the organisation. Which constituents are taken seriously, to the point in some cases of being brought into the decision making structures of the organisation, will depend on various factors. These include the history and stage of development of the organisation, its need for, and possible sources of, legitimacy, the presence of 'competitors' (for funds or for reputation as the leader in the field), the characteristics and 'visibility/vocality' of the constituents themselves, as well as the mission and ethos of the organisation. In the past, and still today, many voluntary organisations have combined a mission of serving consumers with a paternalistic ethos which has effectively ignored service recipients as key constituents. More recently, organisations have responded to the more general emphasis on consumer rights and accountability. In addition, some non-profit organisations have been forced to consider new sources of legitimacy as well as responding to more vocal demands from many disadvantaged groups. For these reasons, among others, some voluntary organisations now include service users on their board/decision-making committees. This practice may create new management problems which are discussed in more detail below.

The second preliminary point is that organisations may be accountable to different groups in different ways. Elsewhere, I have suggested that it is useful to distinguish between three different meanings of accountability. First, explanatory accountability requires that those who are accountable provide an account of their actions, to explain why they acted as they did. The second type – accountability with sanctions – requires that those who are accountable provide an account and those accounted to have the right and the power to impose sanctions on those made accountable. The third type of accountability – responsive accountability – is much weaker; it requires only that those who are accountable in some way respond to the wishes and demands of those to whom they are accountable: they are expected to 'take them into account' (Leat, 1988).

Distinguishing between these different meanings of accountability highlights the way in which organisations may be accountable to different groups in different ways. Some groups may be offered an account or an explanation and others may be merely 'taken into account'. Other groups may, however, have the right to impose sanctions on the organisation if it fails to provide an account and/or fails to comply with their expectations and demands.

Accountability not only has different meanings, it also operates at different levels or in different areas. Here it is worth distinguishing between: fiscal accountability which is about good housekeeping, presenting financial accounts; process accountability which is about how things have been done; and programme accountability which is about what has been achieved. Again different groups may demand or be owed accountability at different levels or in different areas. For example, in the past the Charity Commission has required fiscal accountability from registered charities but very little by way of process and programme accountability.

Accountability of Paid and Unpaid Staff

All organisations demand accountability – explanatory and with sanctions – from their staff. The special problems of staff accountability in many non-profit, and some for-profit, organisations have been discussed elsewhere in this paper. Problems in this regard shared by some non-profit and for-profit organisations include those stemming from the unclear relationship between the Board and paid managers, the preponderance of professionals with specialist knowledge and difficulties in establishing performance measures for all or some staff within the organisation. An egalitarian participative ethos may create further difficulties in relation to accountability with sanctions, perhaps especially in many non-profit organisations. In addition, it was suggested earlier, some non-profit organisations face special problems in relation to the accountability of unpaid volunteers.

Whatever the theory, in many non-profit and for-profit organisations senior management accountability may best be described as, in practice, closer to explanatory accountability than to accountability with sanctions. Senior managers explain to the Board but do not generally expect the Board to apply sanctions. It is worth noting that, in both for-profit and non-profit organisations, when the Board does apply the ultimate sanction of dismissing or suspending senior managers this is 'news'. Lower down the organisation accountability with sanctions may be more relevant, but in some organisations is likely to be constrained by the factors noted above as well as by employment protection legislation.

Centre and Units/Branches

In both for-profit and non-profit organisations the existence of semi-autonomous branches/sub-units may pose problems in reconciling overall standards and accountability with flexibility and a measure of autonomy. Not only do branches have to be accountable to headquarters but, as Moss Kanter notes, increasingly sub-units/branches may demand accountability from headquarters, if only to justify the expense of corporate over-heads (Moss Kanter, 1989). These problems are experienced by for-profit organisations but may be particularly difficult in both for-profit and non-profit organisations when combined with the other problematic features outlined in the previous section.

Members and Accountability

In theory, accountability to members belongs under the heading of 'internal accountability'. In practice, in many non-profit organisations members may be treated as an 'external' group among other groups of constituents which the organisation must satisfy.

As already noted, non-profit organisations vary in structure and in the role and legal rights of members. Non-profit organisation members may or may not have voting rights and to that extent their ability to demand accountability with sanctions varies.

In general, however, it appears that members' theoretical option to demand accountability with sanctions has little real force in practice – at least in influencing the management of the organisation:

> It is perhaps surprising how rarely members were mentioned as a group to which staff saw themselves, or the organisation, as accountable. Members were usually mentioned as an afterthought or were lumped together with 'the community'. The major and for most the only means of accountability to members was via the AGM, at which attendance is usually low.
> (Leat, 1988, p.77).

Thus it seems that in many non-profit organisations members may be treated as people who are owed explanatory accountability at best but are not seriously expected to demand accountability with sanctions. In this respect members of non-profit organisations may be treated much as individual small shareholders are in many for-profit organisations.

There may be two exceptions to the generally weak accountability to members in many non-profit organisations: organisations describing themselves as collectives and organisations whose members are composed primarily of other organisations. In both cases, however, accountability to members may be run together with accountability to members-as-users, much as a for-profit organisation may emphasise accountability to shareholders-as-customers.

For both non-profit and for-profit organisations members/shareholders are important not least because they provide funding as well as, in many cases, legitimacy. For many non-profit organisations, in particular, the larger the membership the more political 'clout' the organisation is likely to have. In some non-profit organisations, especially those which exist to serve other organisations, services may in theory be restricted to those who are members – not least to encourage membership and the subscriptions which more members bring. But this may create dilemmas for some non-profits: given their aim of, for example, serving the disadvantaged or developing the voluntary sector, they cannot restrict their services to members only; on the other hand, if they provide equal rights for members and non-members, why should members pay to join?

> *Our job is providing services that community organisations need. The ones who need our services most are those who are least likely to be members because they're new and small and so on. In that sense they come first. But then we have members who pay a membership fee and to whom we should be more accountable. We get round it by saying anyone can be a user but if you're a member you can vote at the AGM. I'm not sure what it means but it's a formula...* (quoted in Leat, 1988, p.78).

In a similar way, for-profit organisations must seek to satisfy shareholders, customers, potential customers, employees and funders. Similar issues to those raised above regarding accountability to members arise in relation to for-profits' accountability to shareholders.

Information on which company performance can be judged is specified by law requiring disclosure in Directors' Reports, Company Accounts and Balance Sheets. But these are always open to interpretation and in any case do not necessarily provide sufficient information to make judgements. For these and other reasons, the AGM is generally not regarded as an effective instrument of shareholder control. A full understanding of the operation of a modern company would include accountability not only through the AGM but also through the complex network of relationships between shareholders and the financial press, the Stock Exchange and the press and shareholders, managers and the Stock Exchange, as well as potential take-over bidders.

Part of the problem lies in lack of clarity about whose interests the organisation exists to serve, or rather whose interests should be given priority by the Board. In the for-profit sector

> *It is difficult to be precise about the responsibility of directors. Neither Company Law nor the interpretation of it by the courts provides an unambiguous definition. It has been variously interpreted as that of 'trustee, agent and MP' – three very different roles'* (Burningham et al., 1991, p.59).

None of these provide satisfactory models. Furthermore, it is not clear what is meant by 'the company' in whose interests the directors are supposed to act. Studies suggest that directors see shareholders as simply one of the groups, along with customers and employees, to whom they are responsible. Similar ambiguities arise in the non-profit sector.

Accountability to Funders

In both for-profit and non-profit organisations funders may be made up of a variety of groups with very diverse characteristics, demands and expectations. Apart from members, funders of non-profits may include individual donors, corporate donors and central and local government. These broad groups may be further separated into different government departments, different types of corporate donor and different types of individual donor. Each of these sub-constituencies is likely to have different expectations, values and priorities in funding the organisation.

Those who fund an organisation, whether for-profit or nonprofit, are in a special position to demand accountability with sanctions. Their right to require accountability is usually not only legally based, but funders may also apply the sanction of withdrawing financial support. These are genuine stakeholders, rather than simply constituencies. But in both for-profit and non-profit organisations, the real power of their sanction of withdrawing financial support depends on the size of their stake (relative to total organisational income/needs) and on the degree of organisational 'slack'. Thus any one small shareholder in a for-profit or any one individual donor in a non-profit organisation may have little real power/sanction. By contrast, in a for-profit organisation large institutional shareholders or a major lender and, in a non-profit, a major government or corporate funder may possess very real sanctions. Whether or not they exercise these sanctions is another matter.

Arguably, the greater the number of funders who must be satisfied and to whom the organisation must be accountable, the more difficult the management task. But in practice the very number and variety of funders may actually make management's task easier.

First, the greater the number of funders the less likely it is that any one funder will possess real sanctions in relation to the direction and conduct of the organisation. Indeed many nonprofits 'spread' their funding precisely to ensure that this is so.

Secondly, the very variety of funders and their expectations may enable the organisation to claim legitimacy whatever it chooses to do. Thus one course of action may be justified in terms of satisfying individual donors, while another may be justified in terms of satisfying a particular government department. Similarly, in the for-profit organisation customer satisfaction or market penetration may be 'played off' against the short-term profit expectations of shareholders.

There is another reason why a large number of funders and their varying expectations and demands are unlikely to constitute a major constraint on the management of the organisation. Few funders have the time or the knowledge adequately to assess the organisation's performance and this may apply to both large and small stakeholders. Indeed, one reason why government departments fund some voluntary organisations is precisely because they have neither the time nor the specialist knowledge to carry out the activities they fund the organisation to provide. Similarly, in the for-profit organisation small shareholders are not in a position to judge the organisation's performance and, as Robert Maxwell demonstrated, even larger funders such as banks may not be able to do so. And even without deception, the recent study by Terry Smith of accounting practices in the for-profit sector demonstrates that management has the upper hand in how it presents its performance to its funders (Smith, 1992). Furthermore, larger or more expert institutional investors may not have time to enquire too closely into the running of one company which represents only part of a portfolio of shares and securities in a wide number of companies spread across different industries.

Government as Regulator and Funder

All organisations must act within and be accountable in different ways under various laws. For commercial and many nonprofit organisations these are the Companies Acts as well as laws relating to employment practices, public liability and so on. In addition, non-profit organisations which are registered charities must also comply with the Charities Acts and with the directives of the Charity Commission. But, apart from these basic legal requirements, government may also exert demands for accountability and thus constrain the management of both nonprofit and for-profit organisations.

Non-profits, dependent as they often are on substantial amounts of government funding, are sometimes seen as being less independent of government than for-profits. Government funders are, it is implied, a key constituency for non-profits and in some cases actually control them, albeit at arm's length. But on closer inspection non-profits may be rather less different from for-profits in terms of their relationship with government than is sometimes assumed.

First, the idea that non-profits are subsidised by government whereas for-profit organisations are not is not true in Britain. In 1982-83, for example, public expenditure on industry, trade, employment and energy amounted to almost £6 billion (quoted in Lowe and Morgan, 1985). For-profit organisations may be increasingly dependent upon various direct and indirect government subsidies.

Secondly, government exerts influence on for-profit organisations quite independently of any funding it may provide. Meade, a Nobel Prize winner in economics, has summarised the economic grounds for government intervention in for-profit markets. Intervention may be justified on the grounds that it helps: to control and stabilise fluctuations in capital, labour and market products; to control the use of monopoly power by large firms and labour unions; to encourage economies of scale, bringing together enterprises to achieve cost reductions; to provide/facilitate production of 'public goods'; to provide equality of opportunity and rewards; to ensure a long-term benefit (eg control of natural resource depletion); to ensure consideration of social as opposed to economic costs and benefits which the free operation of the commercial market might neglect (eg air pollution) (Meade, 1975). Thus for-profit organisations are 'controlled' by government for reasons and by mechanisms other than funding. The increasing significance of government as a key constituency for for-profit organisations may be reflected in the growth in such organisations of 'government relations' departments.

For-profit organisations, like non-profits, must take government into account as a key constituency but like non-profits they may be differentially constrained, or potentially constrained, in practice. As in the case of non-profits, for-profits' power in relation to their various constituencies, including government, is likely to vary in relation to a number of variables including their size and market position. Larger companies are likely to be more visible and subject to greater government regulation but given their size and resources, they may be able to exert more influence on the nature and form of that intervention. In much the same way larger and more visible non-profit organisations with better 'connections' (eg via Board members) and greater public support may be in a stronger position to influence government policy. Multinational for-profits, and possibly non-profits, may be able both to circumvent regulations by the use of different locations and to exploit the possibility of moving in or out of an area/country as a way of obtaining concessions (Lowe and Morgan, 1985).

Accountability to Users and Customers

One of the virtues non-profit organisations sometimes claim for themselves today is that they are more accountable to their users. In the past, many non-profit organisations were not and did not pretend to be accountable to their users. These were organisations which saw themselves as 'doing good' to others who were not in a position necessarily to know what was good for them. More recently paternalism has given way to professionalism with much the same effect in terms of accountability to users.

One of the many changes in the overall composition of the non-profit sector in the last twenty years or so has been the growth of specifically user-based organisations started by consumers for consumers. For these organisations accountability to users is not an issue because the organisation is composed of users. However, as noted above, as the organisation grows, employs paid staff and moves into other activities, accountability to users may become an increasingly important and difficult issue.

Other organisations have become more consumer-oriented not least because their legitimacy and funding have depended on their doing so. Non-profit organisations have increasingly been used by local authorities to fulfil legal requirements to 'consult the community'. Having neither the time or resources nor the channels of communication to do so themselves, local authorities have turned to voluntary organisations as an easy and available (though not necessarily an appropriate) vehicle for fulfilling their legal responsibilities.

At the same time, however, the notion that market mechanisms – people applying sanctions with their purses – provide the best model of accountability to users has also gained ground. Spurred on by the policies of recent Conservative governments, this notion has led to the creation of markets (in health and social services) where none existed before. According to this view, it is the for-profit organisation which is by definition more accountable to users.

Clearly there is a difference in the extent to which consumers of non-profit and for-profit services may demand accountability with sanctions. Non-profit consumers cannot typically vote with their purses and, even if they could, there is rarely an alternative service. By contrast, in theory, for-profit customers can apply the sanction of withdrawing their custom and going elsewhere.

In practice, however, the differences may be less stark. First, depending on the structure of the market, there may be no ready alternative for both for-profit and non-profit users. Secondly, neither type of user may have adequate information to make a choice. Thirdly, as noted earlier, in both cases there are difficulties in defining the customer, and different types/levels of customer may be able to exert different degrees of sanction on the organisation. Thus it is too simple to say that either type of organisation is more accountable to customers than the other.

What can be said is that both for-profit and non-profit organisations are under increasing pressure to take the views of users into account. Non-profit and for-profit organisations may increasingly include customers/users on decision-making committees. In addition, for-profit organisations may be increasingly constrained by official and unofficial consumer watch-dog groups supposedly representing the interests of users.

In both sectors accountability to users/customers may pose particularly difficult management problems: How are users/customers to be defined and which groups' views should have priority? In for-profit organisations particular problems may arise when customers are also suppliers. How in practice does the organisation obtain the views of different customers and users? How does the organisation reconcile conflicting demands of different groups and/or conflicting demands from the same group? What priority should be given to professional standards and the long-term survival and growth of the organisation as against expressed customer/user preferences? What priority should be given to satisfying the needs of those who are not currently customers/users but are potential users? 'Staying close to the customer' raises difficult issues of principle and practice for both for-profit and non-profit organisations.

Managing with Maximum Visibility

Finally, and more generally, another characteristic of non-profit management sometimes mentioned in the literature is its public visibility. The supposedly greater visibility of non-profit operation and management is linked to non-profit organisations' dependence on individual donors and on publicly accountable government funding.

In addition, registered charities are semi-public bodies both because charitable status requires an element of public benefit and because registration confers certain tax subsidies/benefits. Not offending public notions of appropriate behaviour for charities may have far-reaching implications for the management of such organisations. For example, despite statements by the Charity Commission to the contrary, the general public still appear disposed to believe that money spent on administration is money wasted. Similarly, the general public may also believe that salaries on a par with those in the private sector are inappropriate in charitable organisations.

But whether or not the management of charitable non-profit organisations is, in reality, any more subject to public scrutiny than that of for-profit organisations is debatable. In some cases the management and activities of for-profit organisations may be of more public interest and visibility than those of non-profit organisations which typically attract little detailed attention in the media.

For example, in recent years it has become increasingly common for the pay of senior managers in large commercial organisations to receive considerable public attention – often unfavourable. And recent revelations of company malpractice may serve to whet the appetite of journalists and others, thus increasing public interest and media scrutiny. But the level of public scrutiny experienced by a for-profit organisation is likely to depend on the type of company and its current circumstances. Certainly a company 'in trouble' is likely to have its every move analysed in agonising detail by the media. This happens relatively rarely to non-profit organisations, although in the United States there have been some examples. In some industries and some circumstances commercial company mergers and acquisitions may be the subject of formal public/government investigation and regulation. By contrast, all charity mergers are subject to investigation by the Charity Commission even though such investigations rarely attract much public interest.

Thus the key difference in the visibility of for-profit and non-profit organisations may lie at the level of theory rather than practice. With increasing pressure on for-profit organisations to be more 'socially and environmentally responsible' – pressure often led by non-profit organisations – the activities and management of for-profit organisations may be subject to increasing public scrutiny. In contrast, dissociated from the profit motive and/or basking in the halo of charitable status, non-profit organisations may occupy the moral high ground in the public mind, thus offering some protection from public visibility.

Conclusion

This review has considered the claim that it is possible clearly to differentiate the management of non-profit organisations from that of for-profit organisations. On closer examination, however, those differences which are alleged to exist turn out to be rather less clear cut that is often assumed. In many cases the contrasts are based upon oversimplified views of both types of organisation.

Because both the for-profit and non-profit sectors are internally differentiated, distinctions within the sectors are as important in developing effective management as are those between them. Indeed, the notion of comparing sectors may be less helpful than attempts to identify the management problems of particular types of organisation whether in the non-profit or for-profit sector. It is clearly unhelpful to put ICI and a market stall in the same category (sector) just as it is obvious that Oxfam has little in common with a village playgroup. It may be more illuminating to look at the similarities between, say, Apple and Oxfam than those between, say, Apple and Pepsi. Focusing on organisational types, rather than sector labels, may serve to encourage greater rigour and clarity and discourage over-simplification based on vague differences derived from blanket sectoral stereotypes.

Talk in terms of distinct sectors may, in any case, become increasingly out-dated. As Taylor notes the 1990's are likely to:

> bring profound changes in the voluntary sector and (to) considerable blurring of the boundaries between some voluntary organisations and their counterparts in the statutory and private sectors
> (Taylor, 1991).

As noted in the Introduction to this paper, relationships between the non-profit and for-profit sector are changing fast. Sectoral boundaries are becoming increasingly blurred and there is increasing overlap and interpenetration between organisations as well as growth of hybrid for-profit/non-profit organisations. A further complication, and possible source of confusion and misrepresentation, is the import of the language, methods and approaches of the commercial sector into the non-profit sector. Everyone, in whichever sector, now talks about markets, niches, returns and so on. At the same time, the commercial sector has discovered social goals and values, collegial styles of working, service as the universal goal, the importance of customers/clients coming first as well as the importance of motivators other than money.

Thus this review suggests that attempts to separate off the non-profit sector as a distinct area of study may be misguided. What is needed is a radically different approach focusing on similarities and differences between organisations within and between sectors. This new approach squares with the reality of internal differentiation within the for-profit and non-profit sectors; it also has the advantage of 'going with the policy grain' of increasing integration among statutory, voluntary and commercial organisations.

Relationships Between the Sectors: Convergence?

It has been suggested at various points in this paper that there is increasing convergence of non-profit and for-profit organisations. The reasons for this apparent convergence are complex. On the non-profit side, convergence is related to the growth of contracting, to new resource dependences and to institutional isomorphism. On the for-profit side, convergence may stem from growing disenchantment with existing management practices and a new emphasis on quality and other less tangible values both inside and 'outside' the organisation.

In the new environment of contracting non-profit organisations are becoming more instrumental, more service oriented and more concerned with standards and evaluation. Many are becoming larger, employing more staff, becoming more bureaucratic as well as engaging in more trading and, increasingly, placing more emphasis on charging for their services. As non-profit organisations are becoming more competitive, for-profit organisations are discovering the need for and virtues of cooperative relationships with suppliers and 'competitors'. As non-profit organsations become more managed and bureaucratic, for-profits are emphasising the need for more flexibility, more autonomy, less (old-style) management and more participation. For-profit organisations are discovering intangible goals such as quality and service as well as the need for management by commitment to core values and quality standards. At the same time, non-profit organisations are emphasising cost controls and the need for constant attention to financial viability. If, as Drucker argues, profit is nothing more than the cost of staying in business, then non-profit organisations are becoming more concerned with profit. In addition, both non-profit and for-profit organisations are paying more attention to accountability to stakeholders and constituencies and to more general demands for social responsibility. 'Serving the community' is an ethos no longer monopolised by non-profits and increasingly constitutes part of the rhetoric of many commercial organisations. More generally, the notion that non-profit organisations are characterised by their attempt to optimise multiple values may become increasingly out-dated as for-profit organisations too attempt this delicate balancing act.

Despite this convergence between non-profit and for-profit organisations, there remain differences between them:

> The difficulty lies in expressing the nature and significance of those differences without getting caught up in, or reinforcing, the stereotypes, both positive and negative, of the different sectors (Paton and Cornforth, 1992).

As I have suggested above, however, we are as yet some way from understanding the real nature of these differences as they affect management tasks and needs. The broad and very tentative conclusion of this review is that differences between for-profit and non-profit organisations may be differences of degree and the result of combinations of differences which, although small in themselves, may by their interaction and mutual reinforcement of one another produce real differences in management tasks.

The most fruitful approach in understanding these differences and their combination and interaction may be by comparisons not between the sectors per se but rather between organisations of similar types across sectors. So, for example, it may be fruitful to compare management needs and tasks in for-profit and non-profit organisations with intangible goals and/or a preponderance of professionals/knowledge workers requiring high degrees of autonomy; or the problems of managing non-profit and for-profit organisations with strong traditions of egalitarianism might be considered.

Across the Boundaries

It was suggested in the Introduction to this paper that some non-profit organisations already have experience of the strengths and weaknesses, the practice and unintended consequences, of styles of management which for-profit organisations are now 'discovering'. Conversely, for-profit organisations clearly have considerable experience of many of the practices which non-profit organisations are beginning to adopt. Study of for-profit and non-profit organisations is thus a two-way street in which the traffic of learning flows both ways. In addition, non-profit and for-profit organisations have much to learn together in dealing with common unresolved problems and challenges.

Both types of organisation have much to learn together and from each other about the role of the non-executive Board and the ways in which its composition affects its operation and its effects on managers and management. Finding an effective role for the Board, and the conditions under which this can be achieved, is a challenge for both non-profit and for-profit organisations.

Both types of organisation have much to learn from each other and together in relation to management of staff. Managing professionals and knowledge workers, providing incentives and satisfactions other than purely financial ones, managing by commitment to common core values, building consensus rather than managing by diktat, balancing the autonomy and flexibility necessary for innovation with control, consistency and maintenance of standards – these are management problems faced by non-profit and for-profit organisations alike.

Similarly, non-profit and for-profit organisations face common problems in the proper management of 'branches' and units. How are control and consistency to be combined with autonomy, flexibility and 'space' for innovation? How much central corporate control and expenditure is necessary and justifiable?

For-profit and non-profit organisations have much to learn together in relation to the creation of synergies (Moss Kanter, 1989). Both types of organisation may collect more or less related projects and businesses, but how are these to be managed in a way which creates genuine added value? How is the whole to be made more than the sum of its parts?

In relation to customers, for-profit and non-profit organisations may also learn from each other and together, not least in understanding the variety of customers and the confusion inherent in the very term 'customer'. Study of both types of organisation would permit analysis of the different relationships between producers, funder-customers, immediate customers and end-users/consumers. This sort of study could provide the basis for further analysis of the difficulties of 'staying close to the customer'. Which customers and how may this be achieved? What role should different customers play in influencing product/service development and specification? And so on.

Similarly, non-profit and for-profit organisations may be able to learn from each other and together in understanding and developing supplier-customer (contractor) relationships. What role and responsibility should suppliers play in contract specification? What are the problems and effects of more equal, co-operative approaches to supplier-customer/contractor relationships? What are the implications of, and limits to, putting genuine power into supplier-customer relationships? How are issues of organisational autonomy and organisational dependence, on both sides, handled?

Finally, non-profit and for-profit organisations face similar challenges in responding appropriately to demands for greater accountability by and to staff, funders, customers and users, branches/units, government and 'society' generally. What are the implications of these demands from different stakeholders and wider constituencies for the efficient and effective management of the organisation? What priority should be given to each? What are the proper limits to 'social responsibilities' and are these consistent with both for-profit and non-profit organisations' accountabilities and responsibilities to their prime constituencies? How may tensions and conflicts in such responsibilities be balanced?

These are just some of the common challenges facing managers of both for-profit and non-profit organisations. Study of organisations across the two sectors would no doubt identify others. Study of non-profit organisations alongside that of for-profit organisations would indeed create synergies adding value to our theoretical and practical understanding of the management of different types of for-profit and non-profit organisations operating under different conditions and constraints.

References

Adirondack, S. (1989), *Just About Managing*, London Voluntary Service Council, London.

Austin, M. and Posnett, J. (1979), The Charity Sector in England and Wales – Characteristics and Public Accountability, *National Westminster Bank Quarterly*, August.

Ball, C. (1992), 'Remuneration Policies and Employment Practices: Some Dilemmas in the Voluntary Sector', in J. Batsleer *et al*.

Balloun, J.S. (1981), Real lessons from Japan, *Speaking of Japan*, 13.

Batsleer, J., Cornforth, C. and Paton, R. (eds) (1992), *Issues in Voluntary and Non-profit Management*, Open University/Addison Wesley Publishing Co., London.

Baumol, W.J. (1959), *Business Behaviour, Value and Growth*, Macmillan, London.

Billis, D. (1990), 'Planned Change in Voluntary and Government Social Service Agencies', in *Towards the 21st Century Challenges for the Voluntary Sector*, Proceedings of the 1990 Conference of the Association of Voluntary Action Scholars, CVO, London.

Blau, P.M. and Scott, R.W. (1962), *Formal Organizations: A Comparative Approach*, Chandler, San Francisco.

Bruce, I. and Raymer, A. Managing and Staffing Britain's Largest Charities, VOLPROF, City University Business School.

Burningham, D. *et al* (1991), *Economics*, Hodder and Stoughton, London.

Butler, R.J. and Wilson, D.C. (1990), *Managing Voluntary and Non-profit Organisations*, Routledge, London.

Charities Aid Foundation (1991), *Charity Trends, 14th Edition*, CAF, Tonbridge.

Clark, P.B. and Wilson, J.Q. (1961), Incentive Systems: A Theory of Organizations, *Administrative Science Quarterly*, 6: 129-166.

Day, R. (1991), 'Survey of Staffing Levels in the Top 400 Fundraising Charities', in *Charity Trends*.

DiMaggio, P. and Powell, W.W. (1983), 'The Iron Cage Revisited: Institutional Isomorphism and Collective Rationality in Organizational Fields', *American Sociological Review*, 48: 147-160.

Drucker, P. (1964), *Managing For Results*, William Heinemann, London.

Drucker, P. (1977), *Management*, Harpers College Press, New York.

Drucker, P. (1968), *The Practice of Management*, Pan Books, London.

Drucker, P. (1985), *Innovation and Entrepreneurship*, William Heinemann, London.

Drucker, P. (1988), The Coming of the New Organization, *Harvard Business Review*, Jan-Feb, pp 45-53.

Drucker, P. (1989), What business can learn from non-profits, *Harvard Business Review*, July-Aug, pp 89-93.

Drucker, P. (1990), *Managing the Non-profit Organization*, Butterworth Heineman, London.

Elliott, K. and Lawrence, P. (eds) (1985), *Introducing Management*, Penguin, Harmondsworth.

Gordon, C.W. and Babchuk, N. (1959), A Typology of Voluntary Associations, *American Sociological Review*, 24, 22-29.

Gouldner, A.W. (1969), The Secrets of Organisations in R.M. Kramer and H. Specht (eds), *Readings in Community Organization Practice*, Prentice Hall Inc, Englewood Cliffs, New Jersey.

Handy, C. (1988), *Understanding Voluntary Organisations*, Penguin.

Hansen, H. (1976), *The British Manager*, Harvard University Press, Boston.

Haspeslaugh, P. (1982), Portfolio planning, uses and limits, *Harvard Business Review*, 60, 1, Jan/Feb. 58-73.

Hansmann, H.B. (1981), Why are non-profit organizations exempted from corporate income taxation?, in M.J. White (ed) *Non-Profit Firms in a Three Sector Economy*, Urban Institute, Washington D. C.: 115-134.

Harris, M. (1992), 'The Role of Voluntary Management Committees', in Batsleer *et al.*

Knapp, M. and Kendal, J. (1991), Mapping the Voluntary Sector, *Charity Trends 14th Edition*.

Kramer, R. (1965), Ideology, Status and Power in Board Executive Relationships, *Social Work*, 10: 107-14.

Leat, D., Smolka, G. and Unell, J. (1981), *Voluntary and Statutory Collaboration: Rhetoric or Reality?*, Bedford Square Press, London.

Leat, D. (1988), *Voluntary Organisations and Accountability*, NCVO, London.

Lee, B. (1985), Internal Politics, in Elliott and Lawrence.

Lowe, J. and E.J. Morgan, (1985), Government Policy and the Economic System, in Elliott and Lawrence.

Marris, R. (1964), *The Economic Theory of Managerialism*, Macmillan, London.

Mason, D. (1984), *Voluntary Nonprofit Enterprise Management*, Plenum Press, New York.

Mason, D. (1991), Non-profits Well Managed, in *Towards the 21st Century – Challenges for the Voluntary Sector*, Proceedings of the 1990 Conference of the Association of Voluntary Action Scholars, CVO, London.

Meade, J.E. (1975), *The Intelligent Radicals' Guide to Economic Policy*, Allen and Unwin, London.

Michels, R. (1949), *Political Parties*, Free Press, Glencoe, IL.

Middleton, M. (1987), Nonprofit Boards of Directors: Beyond the Governance Function, in Powell.

Moss Kanter, R. (1989), *When Giants Learn to Dance*, Simon and Schuster, London.

Moss Kanter, R. and Summers, D.V. (1987), Doing Well While Doing Good: Dilemmas of Performance Measurement in Non-profit Organizations and the Need for a Multiple-Constituency Approach, in Powell.

Mullin, R. (1980), *Present Alms*, Phlogiston Publishing, Birmingham.

Paton, R. and Cornforth, C. (1992), What's Different about Managing in Voluntary and Non-profit Organizations? in Batsleer *et al.*

Peters, T. and Austin, N. (1985), *A Passion for Excellence*, William Collins, London.

Peters, T. and Waterman, R. (1982), *In Search of Excellence*, Harper and Row, New York.

Powell, W.W. (ed) (1987), *The Nonprofit Sector; A Research Handbook*, Yale University Press, New Haven, CT.

Powell, W.W. and Friedkin, R. (1987), Organizational Change in Nonprofit Organizations, in Powell.

Rose, A. (1967), *The Power Structure: Political Process in American Society*, Oxford University Press, New York.

Rowe, A. (1978), Participation and the Voluntary Sector: The Independent Contribution, *Journal of Social Policy*, 7, (1).

Salamon, L. (1987), Partners in Public Service: The Scope and Theory of Government-Nonprofit Relations, in Powell.

Saxon-Harrold, S. (1990), Competition, Resources and Strategy in the British Nonprofit Sector, in H.K. Anheier and W. Seibel (eds), *The Third Sector: Comparative Studies of Nonprofit Organizations*, Walter de Gruyter, Berlin and New York.

Scott, J. (1985), Ownership, Management and Strategic Control, in Elliott and Lawrence.

Scully, J. (1987), *Odyssey Pepsi to Apple*, Fontana, London.

Selznick, P. (1960), *The Organizational Weapon: A Study of Bolshevik Strategy and Tactics*, Free Press, Glencoe, IL.

Senor, J.M. (1965), Another Look at the Executive Board Relationship, in M.N. Zald (ed) *Social Welfare Institutions, A Sociological Reader*, John Wiley and Sons, Chichester.

Shipley, D.D. (1981), Primary objectives in British manufacturing industry, *Journal of Industrial Economics*, 29, 4 June.

Sills, D. (1957), *The Volunteers*, Free Press, Glencoe, IL.

Sizer, J. (1982), Pricing and product profitability analysis, *Management Accounting (UK)*, 60, 2 Feb.

Smith, T. (1992), *Accounting for Growth*, Century Business, London.

Stanton, E. (1970), *Clients Come Last: Volunteers and Welfare Organizations*, Sage Publications Inc.

Taylor, M. (1991), *New Times, New Challenges, Voluntary Organisations Facing 1990*, National Council for Voluntary Organisations, London.

Volunteer Centre UK (1991), *The 1991 National Survey of Voluntary Activity*, Volunteer Centre UK, Berkhamsted.

Walton, R.E. and Susman, G.I. (1987), People Policies for the New Machines, *Harvard Business Review*, March-April (2): 98-106.

Ware, A. (1989), *Between Profit and State, Intermediate Organizations in Britain and the United States*, Polity Press, Cambridge.

White, M. (1985), Japanese Management, in Elliott and Lawrence.

Williamson, O.E. (1963), Managerial discretion and business behaviour, *American Economics Review*, 53, Dec.

Willis, E. (1992), Managing Volunteers, in Batsleer *et al.*

Wilson, D. (1989), New Trends in the Funding of Charities: the tripartite system of funding, in A. Ware (ed), Charities and Government, Manchester University Press, Manchester.

Young, D.R. (1985), What Business Can Learn From Nonprofits, *Models of Health and Human Services in the Nonprofit Sector*, Association of Voluntary Action Scholars.

Young, D.R. (1987), Executive Leadership in Nonprofit Organizations, in Powell.

Young, D.R. and Finch, S.J. (1977), *Foster Care and Nonprofit Agencies*, Lexington Books, Lexington.